**FIND
YOUR
RED
THREAD**

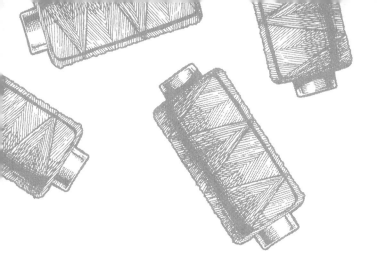

Make Your Big Ideas Irresistible

FIND
YOUR
RED
THREAD

(**TAMSEN WEBSTER**)

●● **PAGE TWO** BOOKS

Cataloguing in publication information is
available from Library and Archives Canada.
ISBN 978-1-77458-052-3
ISBN 978-1-77458-053-0

Various terms used throughout this book are trademarked.
These include the Red Thread®, Fear Experiments™,
Multi-Level Leadership™, Marketing Agility Ascension™,
Red Thread Storyline™, and Red Thread Throughline™.

Page Two
pagetwo.com

Edited by Kendra Ward
Copyedited by Tilman Lewis
Cover and interior design by Peter Cocking

tamsenwebster.com

"WORDS, MADEMOISELLE, ARE
ONLY THE OUTER CLOTHING OF IDEAS."

AGATHA CHRISTIE, *The ABC Murders*

CONTENTS

THE FOOL
WANDERS,
THE WISE MAN
TRAVELS

INTRODUCTION

T HIS BOOK could have been one sentence: *The best way to make your idea irresistible is to build the story people will tell* themselves *about it.*

In fact, if you already know how to do that (or if your idea is already irresistible), you can probably stop reading now. I'm grateful you picked up this book, but it's not for you.

If, instead, you see that your idea is so powerful that it could change a life, a market, or even the world, but others don't see it . . . *yet*—then I wrote this book for you. I wrote it for people, like you, who want their idea to impact the world. I wrote it for people, like you, who value the possibility of their idea so much that they see it as bigger than they are; who are willing to put the *idea* first. I wrote it for people, like you, who, despite their motivation and willingness to do the work, struggle to communicate how irresistible their idea really is.

I've already told you what to do: build the story people will tell themselves about your idea. This technique, which you'll learn how to do in the pages ahead, is called the Red Thread.

Making Ideas Make Sense

In Sweden and other northern European countries, the expression "red thread" refers to the core idea of something, the "throughline" that makes it all make sense. You'd say it when you're trying to clarify what something means. You could ask, "What's the red thread here?" And the answer might be, "Our red thread is to drive not just action, but long-term change." In other words, you'd use this expression to get to the bottom of questions like the ones you probably get about your idea: "What is it?" "What is it about?" And underneath all those: "Why should I care?"

Your idea—your product, your brand, your business, your service—has a red thread. It is the mental path you took to make sense of your idea. And if you want your idea to inspire action and real, lasting change, it has to make sense to other people, as well. They have to see the red thread in it. They have to hear your red thread in your answer to their questions about your business, product, or brand when they land on your website, when they talk with you in a sales meeting or pitch presentation, when they hear from you in an online video or at a conference keynote. Most of all? They have to understand and agree with your idea. They need that red thread as their guide through the maze of other ideas and options, and through the maze of their own heads. The red thread will inspire them to act in the way you want them to, to get the outcome you're looking for.

The expression "red thread" comes from the story of a mythic hero—a slayer of monsters and a master of mazes. You'll soon see that you are a modern-day version of this hero.

First, though, you have to find what I'll call, capitalized, the Red Thread of your idea.

That's the Red Thread this book is all about. It is a clear, powerful answer to the most important aspects of your idea: what it is, and why people should care. I'll lay out a process to make sure your idea is as strong as it can be, by answering all the questions your audience (clients, customers, investors) are asking about it, both consciously and not.

How to Use This Book

The biggest obstacle to inspiring your audience to act is the gap between what you want to say about your idea and what people need to hear about it. To be inspired to act, the human brain needs to hear a specific structure, and it all comes down to story. In this book, you'll learn how to use five core elements of story structure to express the core elements of your idea itself and any case you need to make for it.

Find Your Red Thread has three main parts. In the first, Context, I explain the story of the red thread of

GREAT IDEAS
AREN'T FOUND,
THEY'RE BUILT.

———

Swedish idiom and the Red Thread this book is all about. I also introduce you to the five core elements of story you'll be working with throughout the rest of the book:

* Establishing a GOAL
* Introducing a PROBLEM someone didn't know they had
* Discovering a TRUTH that demands a choice
* Defining a CHANGE in thinking or behavior
* Describing the ACTION, or actions, that will make that change concrete

You'll start drafting your own Red Thread by identifying where you'll use it, with whom, and to what hoped-for end.

In the second part, Components, we'll get into the details of each of the five "Red Thread statements": specific, templated sentences about these goal, problem, truth, change, and action elements of your story. Each chapter includes a definition of the element, the criteria for that statement, and step-by-step guidance for developing it. You'll also see a chapter on the goal revisited meant to bring your work on your Red Thread full circle.

The chapters in the final part, Combinations, show you how to combine Red Thread statements into the forms I and my clients have found most useful: one-paragraph summaries called your Red Thread Storyline, which string together all your work on your Red Thread statements, and a one-sentence summary called a Red Thread Throughline (like the one that started this book). Finally, the conclusion reveals two additional interpretations and applications of your Red Thread, and a third that may be the most important one of all: how finding the Red Thread of your idea may help you find the Red Thread of you.

Where and How to Use Your Red Thread

I've tested the approach you're about to learn with hundreds of ideas and hundreds of clients, including the most skeptical and story-phobic. (I'm looking at you, scientists and engineers!) I've taught it to thousands more. People have used the Red Thread method to build communications as varied as these:

* Marketing messages and materials
* Strategic sales conversations
* Pitches and internal presentations
* Public presentations like keynotes, breakout sessions, and multi-part workshops
* Fundraising asks
* Books and online content

The results? My clients (and others) have used the Red Thread to raise millions of dollars for their research or for their start-ups or other organizations. Dozens of companies have used it to frame the basis of their internal and market positioning. It's also provided the starting outline for multiple books, including bestsellers, and for hundreds of presentations that range from internal update meetings to keynotes and TED and local TEDx talks (10 million-plus YouTube views and counting). So, yes, it helps you get the impact you envision for your idea.

Throughout the book, you'll see a series of examples drawn from this work. Those examples will introduce the following Red Threads (always in this order):

- A life science start-up called UrSure, which wanted to improve its investor pitch.

- Ethnologist Tricia Wang, who wanted to build a TEDx talk strong enough to be a featured talk on TED.com.[1] (It was! And, as of this writing, the same has happened with six others of my clients.)

- A nonprofit media company's editorial and fund-raising teams, which needed executive team buy-in (and financial support) for a new project.

- Author, speaker, and coach Linda Ugelow, who wanted to draft a keynote that would serve as the basis of a book (which it did).

- Career coach and career clarity expert Tracy Timm, who wanted to diversify her message to a new audience.

- Speaker, author, and former Second City member Judi Holler, who wanted to revise her current key-note to command higher fees and bigger stages.

- Leadership strategist, author, and speaker Ted Ma, who wanted to differentiate his leadership message from others in the marketplace.

One more thing: as you read, look for the Red Thread–based summaries that start each chapter. They are the bones on which I built that particular chapter and this book as a whole. So this book is itself an example of the Red Thread method at work, and of how you can use it to build on your big idea, too.

Building the Unique, Universal Story

Great ideas aren't found, they're built—piece by piece, on a unique but universal story. Your story connects how you uniquely see the world with how you uniquely do what you do in it. Your story forms a Red Thread that you unwittingly follow every day.

Without a Red Thread, your story isn't clear—to you or to anyone else. But with it, each piece of the story, the idea, takes shape, and suddenly, how you see the world changes, often forever. That's the fabled "Eureka!" moment of Archimedes in his bathtub or Sir Isaac Newton with his apple. It's the moment you see a new way to slay your monster. It's the moment you know you can make change happen.

But it's also a universal story, one that everyone's brain follows and recognizes. Because of that, it's possible to tell your idea's story in that universal form, to build that Red Thread in someone else's mind, whether in a casual conversation or over the course of a book.

Then they, like you, can have that same moment. They can suddenly see how to slay *their* monster *your* way. Your idea becomes theirs.

That's the power, and the possibility, of the Red Thread. The thing I hear most often from people who use it to drive action from their ideas? "It just works."

Let's make it work for you.

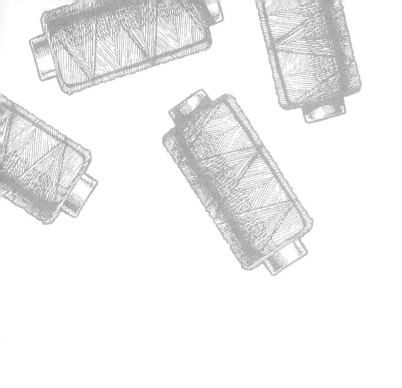

PART

1

CONTEXT

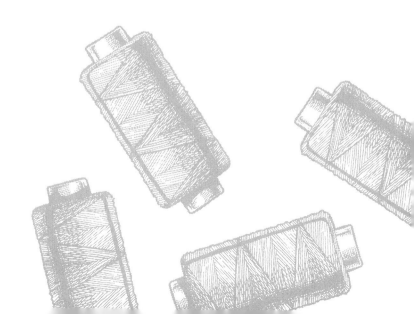

GOOD TUNES
ARE PLAYED ON
OLD FIDDLES

(1)

THE STORY OF THE RED THREAD

GOAL: Turn your idea into action (and maybe even change the world).

PROBLEM: There's a big difference between what you want to say about your idea and what other people need to hear. People need to understand—and agree with—your idea before they'll act on it.

TRUTH: The human brain has a specific structure for how it processes, accepts, and acts on ideas: story. Ideas are built on stories.

CHANGE: For your idea to truly drive action—and lasting change—you need to build a story that people will tell themselves about your idea.

ACTION: To build that story, find the story your brain built about your idea in the first place. That story is your Red Thread.

A Tool for Every Task

Both the Red Thread we're talking about in this book and the idiomatic one get their name from the solution to a very old puzzle: how to defeat the Minotaur of Greek myth. For one man, Theseus, it was critical to solve that puzzle. As the future king of Athens, he needed to slay the half-man, half-bull monster to save his city.

But that wasn't the only problem he had to solve. Even if Theseus could kill the Minotaur, he would have to escape the labyrinth where it lived. The challenge: the labyrinth was so dark and so complicated that even the Minotaur itself couldn't escape. For Theseus, the maze was just as important as the monster.

So, what did Theseus do? He brought a tool for each task. To kill the monster, he carried a sword. To master the maze, he brought a ball of red thread. With the thread, he traced his path to the monster so that he could retrace his path on the way out. He slayed the monster. He saved his city.

What does that have to do with your business, your brand, your offering—in other words, with your idea? As it turns out, pretty much everything. After all, the best ideas are often those that find a new way to solve an old problem (slay the monster) or achieve a desired goal (save the city). They create a change in thinking, on scales both large and small. And yet, where those great, change-making ideas come from (and how to spread them) too often remains as dark and complicated as the legendary labyrinth.

Hearing (or reading or seeing) the Red Thread of an idea is key to your audience (your customers, clients, funders—or anyone else you want to influence) acting on it. Before you can show your audience, though, you must find it for yourself. Just as Theseus did, you need to retrace your steps—all the way back to the beginning of your idea.

What Is an Idea, Anyway?

Once upon a time, you (or your company) asked a question: "How can we...?" "What if we...?" "Why haven't we...?" Like Theseus, you had a monster to slay. You asked that starting question because you saw a problem to solve, a need to meet, or a goal to achieve.

With that question in mind, you sought an answer. You looked at the situation. You probably studied it. You saw other answers to the question. You may even have tried some of those answers. For whatever reason, though, those answers just weren't "right," at least not for you. But then, one day, something changed. You found another way to think about the problem, or you noticed something you hadn't seen before. Once you did, though, it probably seemed so obvious to you that you wondered why you hadn't noticed before, or why no one else had, either! Whatever the case, something clicked. The light bulb went on. And you got it: an idea for what to do differently. You knew how to answer that original question in a way that no one else ever had before.

Maybe the process was a bit slower. Perhaps the question wasn't a conscious one; it just started as nameless searching. Maybe the answer didn't strike you like lightning—you just slowly started to do things the way you do them now. But I'll still bet there was a moment when you looked around and saw that your way was new. And different. And better.

That's an idea. An idea is an answer, your answer, to a question that doesn't already have an answer or that needs a better one.

Your idea is your new way to slay a monster that needs fighting. Other people could use it, too, to slay the same monster—if only they knew how. Take, for example, the virtual chat service Slack. It was a new way for companies to communicate with each other, and it solved the problems of email—which itself was once a new way to solve the problems of paper memos and meetings. TED speaker Simon Sinek's "Start with Why"[2] was a new way for leaders to think about how to "inspire action." And once upon a time a diamond ring was a new way for couples to show their commitment was "forever." (More on that last one soon.)

You, too, have an idea, and your next step is to let people know about it. But that's where the trouble starts.

STORY IS
THE MAP OF
THE MAZE.

Where Ideas Fail First, and Fast

You've probably heard of TED talks. They're a series of three- to eighteen-minute talks about "ideas worth spreading" that you can watch online. They're one of the many ways people like you get their ideas out into the wider world.

I spent four years as the executive producer of TEDxCambridge, the oldest and one of the largest locally organized events building on the TED talk brand. As part of that role, and as part of my current one as the event's idea strategist, I review aspiring speakers' applications. Right at the beginning of that application, speakers have to answer this challenge: "Explain your idea in a single sentence of 140 characters or less."

And I have to tell you, most speakers' TEDx talk dreams die right there. Why? Because most of them can't do it. At least, they can't explain their idea in a way that helps us, the organizers, understand it or want to explore it further. They can't help us see why their idea is a new and potentially better way to answer an important question or slay an age-old monster. Out of hundreds of applications, we have only ever seen *one* that met that standard right out of the gate.

Think about that: the applicants are highly accomplished scientists and scholars. Most of the time they want to talk about the product of their life's work. No one knows more about their ideas than they do. They have *all* the answers. And yet, they can't explain them. At least not concisely, or even comprehensibly. Often, when reviewing the applications, my fellow reviewers and I can't figure out what the speaker's idea even is! More critically, we can't figure out why we (or our audience) should care.

I've seen the same phenomenon repeatedly in business, too. For twenty-five years now, I've worked in brand and message strategy, with a huge variety of organizations. Nonprofits and for-profits. Start-up companies. Fortune 500 companies, all the way up to companies in the Fortune 10.

I also see it with my individual clients. Founders, researchers, thought leaders.

Over and over again, great, important ideas never make it out of their creators' heads. The ideas die the moment people have to explain them to an audience.

Why? Because it's not enough to have an idea, even if it's great. It's not enough to know how to slay the monster in new and better ways. You need something more than that. You need people to navigate the twists and turns of their own understanding and agreement. So, you have to show people how to get through the maze, just like Theseus used his red thread to get through the labyrinth. It's the only way they'll act, and the only way your idea—and all you hope and dream for it—will survive.

We'll talk more about that maze soon, but first, let's talk about your idea.

The "TEDx Test": What Is Your Idea?

I get it. You may be thinking that none of this applies to you. If you read my warning at the beginning of the book and decided to keep reading anyway, you may feel that your idea is already so great and so clear that people immediately see its brilliance (and yours). Even the merest hint of your idea is enough to change people's minds and lives forever.

Maybe so. But let's find out for sure, shall we? Let's put your idea to the "TEDx test."

Grab something to write with. Now, imagine you're standing with someone whom you don't just want to act on your idea, but you *need* them to. Someone like your prospective client. Or an investor. Or a publisher. And they know nothing about your idea. Imagine you strike up a conversation and they ask you this question: "So, what is your idea?"

→ **DO THIS**: Write down your answer to that question, as you'd say it out loud.

Don't just think your idea through in your head (because your head will lie to you). Write. It. Down.

I'll wait.

Okay, got it?

Now, looking at what you wrote, answer these questions:

* Is it one sentence?

* Is it 140 characters or less?

* Does it use only words that someone who knows nothing about your idea would easily understand?

* Does it include something your audience wants?

* Would your audience agree that they want it? out loud? in front of colleagues or friends?

* Does it include something they haven't heard before?

To know whether or not your idea is clear enough, relevant enough, remarkable enough for someone to be interested enough to learn more, you need to ask these questions. To give your idea a fighting chance, you must get a "yes" to each one. If you answered "no" to any of them, then it's very likely the people you're talking to would get lost in the maze that surrounds your idea. Which means, they wouldn't want to know more. They certainly wouldn't act. They'd likely just nod politely and move on.

Take heart, though. By the end of this book, you should be so thoroughly acquainted with this process and your idea that you will be able to craft a crisp, concise, and compelling statement with the power to move your audience to act. I call that your Red Thread Throughline.

The Maze of the Mind

Here's the bad news: according to Harvard Business School professor Gerald Zaltman, 95 percent of our decision-making is unconscious.[3] It happens "in the dark," without us even realizing we've done it. The same is likely true for your idea. Even when you're looking for a new idea or innovation, you don't really spend time thinking about how you think about it. Your brain just feeds you messages that tell you, "Yes, that's it!" or "No, try again."

Here's why: when you're trying to solve problems, achieve goals, and find new answers to old questions, your brain is navigating a maze you can't see but you can usually feel. You feel it when your mind keeps spinning on an unsolved problem or when the answer is just ... out ... of ... reach. The fact that you can't see that maze is why, when the proverbial light bulb suddenly turns on, it seems so surprising.

You know the answer is right, but how did you get there?

Understanding that journey is critical, because that's what people want to know about your idea. "How did you get there?" is what people mean when they ask why you think your idea is the right one, and especially the right one for them.

The problem is that we tend to answer that question from the perspective of having already gone through the maze. In fact, because so much of the maze was hidden from view, most of us don't even realize we were in it in the first place. This, my friends, is why so many ideas fail. We're trying to tell people how to slay the monster, but we're telling them as someone who has already navigated the maze successfully. From the perspective of an expert.

That expert perspective is, sadly, a curse. And not just metaphorically. The "curse of knowledge" is the name that economists and, later, psychologists gave to the idea that "once we know something, we find it hard to imagine what it was like not to know it."[4]

Your audience doesn't know what you know, though. They may hear you telling them you've solved their problem. They can definitely hear that you're sure the solution is great. But there's a big difference between being told something is the right answer and discovering it for yourself, especially when the information is new. As mathematician Blaise Pascal once said, "People are generally better persuaded by reasons which have come into their own mind than those from the minds of others."[5] In other words, people don't just want the answer. They want *their* answer. They need to find their own way to your idea.

If you give them a Red Thread, that's exactly what they'll do.

Take one of my start-up clients, Solstice, and their audience, a community in California. Solstice works in community solar, which offers a way for groups of people to reap the benefits of solar power—lower energy prices and positive environmental effects—without individuals having to invest individually in solar panels and related equipment. Solstice's audience was asking of them, "How does this help me save money on my utility bills?" The challenge for Solstice was that *how* community solar achieves those benefits is fairly complicated, and the promise—lower energy bills with no risk—sounded too good to be true.

But, by introducing a simple, familiar analogy—carpooling—we helped potential Solstice customers understand the *idea* of how community solar works: When you want to save money, there's (literally) power in numbers. When a group of people share solar resources, they get the benefits at a lower cost. Our approach helped potential Solstice customers connect their question ("How does this help me save on utility bills?") to an answer that makes sense to them: "'Carpool' with my neighbors on solar energy costs." Solstice is the way they can do that.

Convincing someone of your idea, particularly if it's a big departure from current thinking or behavior, often means asking for a big "yes," too. That's where the Red Thread comes in. Rather than expecting (or hoping) your audience will somehow, all on their own, navigate the journey to saying yes to your idea, your Red Thread will give them, and their brains, a map to follow. Importantly, it also gives them a way to say yes to much smaller concepts first. You'll break up that big mental trip into much smaller—and to their brains, safer—stages.

The Universal Map: Story

At this point, you may be thinking, "Wait a minute. I'm supposed to give people a guide through a maze I traveled through but don't remember and can't see?"

Yep. That's the bad news. But here's the good news: there's one path through the maze that always works.

See, a huge portion of what happens in that unconscious 95 percent of decision-making is known: We know how the brain makes sense of new information. We know what it's looking for. We know how it processes what it finds. We have a map for it. Story.

Story is the map of the maze.

When presented with new information, your brain processes it as a story. It identifies the characters. It assigns them motivations. It predicts results based on what it already knows about the world. Importantly, your brain does this even when the information isn't told as a "Once upon a time" kind of story. Filling in the blanks of a story is simply how you make sense of the world. "Why did this good thing happen to me? Because I worked hard!" (I'm the hero!) "Why did this bad thing happen? Because that person has a grudge against me!" (He's a villain!)

Here's even better news: Because you now know that fact about the brain, you have an opportunity you didn't have before—to make sure you can answer the questions your audience asks out loud (like "What is your idea?" and "Why should I care about it?") as well as the unconscious questions that determine whether or not they are satisfied with your answer.

What are those unconscious questions? Thankfully, that's known, too. Research studying the brains of infants and young children[6] through those of grown adults shows that we pay attention to, learn, and remember the same types of concepts.[7] More specifically, we pay attention to people (characters), what they do (actions), why (motivations), and what happens as a result (effects). As it turns out, those elements are also the main elements of stories! Our brains are wired to ask questions that help us create a story that makes sense to us.

But don't worry! You don't have to become a storytelling (or neuroscience) expert to figure out how to effectively and meaningfully share your ideas with your audience. The simple structure that I'll take you through, step by step, will answer all of your audience's questions—conscious and unconscious—and create your Red Thread.

Simplifying Story Structure

There are probably as many ways to describe and build a story as there are stories. Google "How do I build a story?" and you'll find a range of (mostly unhelpful) answers. You may have already heard one of the simplest answers, that a story "has a beginning, middle, and end." Well, to paraphrase a storytelling colleague of mine, so does a piece of string![8] Just knowing what a story "has" doesn't tell you how to build one.

You also may have heard of the Hero's Journey, the famed "monomyth" or universal story, so named because it appears again and again throughout history, in almost every culture and era. The challenge, at least to me and the busy people I work with, is that most people have neither the time nor the patience to define and fulfill all twelve(!) steps of it. Plus, as familiar and powerful as it may be, the Hero's Journey isn't the basis of *all* stories, so its application is, by definition, limited. Even though the hero myth is a story your brain enjoys hearing, it isn't the story your brain automatically tries to build—your brain is looking for something much simpler.

To figure out how to build *that* kind of story, I sought answers from all corners of story and storytelling: fiction and nonfiction writing, screenwriting and play-writing, public speaking and presenting, marketing and sales messaging, neuroscience, learning theory, behavioral economics, you name it. I read thousands of pages. I tested dozens of tools and models, not just on my own ideas, but on my TEDx speakers' and clients' ideas, as well.

My goal? Find a way to structure a story that would

- be simple enough for busy people to learn, remember, and apply easily,

- be flexible enough to cover multiple applications, and

- still capture the most critical elements, and benefits, of story.

Spoiler alert: I didn't find one.
So I built one, instead.
Remember those elements of story I mentioned earlier? The ones researchers have found that we all remember because they're what help us make sense of the world? I combined that research with my own into the most common elements of great stories and found they overlapped. There are surely any number of ways

to characterize the common elements of both "brain" stories and "storytelling" stories. Based on my experience, the Red Thread is the simplest way to combine them into one set.

After testing my approach with hundreds of clients (and, at this point, millions of audience members), I've simplified the core story elements to these five, in this order:

* Establishing a GOAL—the action of a story begins when we discover what someone wants.

* Introducing a PROBLEM someone didn't know they had—this creates conflict and tension, which is the engine of all action.

* Discovering a TRUTH that makes inaction impossible, because it puts the goal in jeopardy. (In stories, this is often referred to as the "moment of truth," the "midpoint," or the "climax.") This discovery forces a person to choose something.

* Deciding to CHANGE—this is what happens as a result of the truth, and it determines whether or not the ending is happy.

* Turning the change into ACTION—this is what someone does to make the change real.

Goal. Problem. Truth. Change. Action. These five elements are the answers to the questions your brain—everyone's brain—asks about ideas. They are what everyone's brain needs to hear and understand for an idea to make sense, for it to find the red thread of Swedish idiom.

Goal. Problem. Truth. Change. Action. These five factors are what your brain—everyone's brain—needs to register to build the story they'll tell themselves to understand, agree with, and act on your idea.

Goal. Problem. Truth. Change. Action. Those five keys are what *you* need to find, and give to your audience, to turn your idea into action.

So, now it's time for the best news of all: *You already have the answers for your own idea*. Why? Because your story-seeking brain already asked and answered those questions about your idea. Your idea is the result of a story your brain built to get there.

Every idea has a story because every idea is a story. That story is the Red Thread. It's time to get started on yours.

Steps Through the Maze (aka Action Items!)

To start finding your Red Thread, have you:

☐ Written out your answer to "What is your idea?" as you'd say it out loud? (Keep this answer handy—you'll need it later!)

(2)

APPLICATION, OUTCOME, AND AUDIENCE

GOAL: Build the story of change people will tell themselves (so you can turn your idea into action, and maybe even change the world).

PROBLEM: Your idea has and is a story, but stories and ideas aren't the same. There's always more than one way to talk about your idea.

TRUTH: Situation drives story. What you say about your idea depends on whom you're talking to and what you want to achieve.

CHANGE: Find the story that suits the situation.

ACTION: Define the application, outcome, and audience of your idea.

WHEN THE MUSIC CHANGES, SO DOES THE DANCE

One Idea, Infinite Stories

If you want to drive action, you need to build the story people will tell themselves about your idea. You know your idea has a story because your idea is a story—the story your brain built about it in the first place. But there's more than one way to tell that story.

You've no doubt heard a phrase like "all dogs are animals, but not all animals are dogs." The same is true for stories and ideas. You may have one idea, but you have multiple stories, multiple messages, to tell about it. As the great author Agatha Christie once wrote, "Words . . . are only the outer clothing of ideas." But whether you turn your idea into a product or service or book, you have to talk or write about it first.

Sadly, words are a poor proxy for the big, beautiful ideas in your head. No matter how well-chosen they are, words never perfectly capture all that your idea is, does, and can be. You can get close, though, and that's where your message comes in.

Your message is the words you need to say to an audience about your idea to achieve a particular outcome.

I often tell clients: Think about your job. Imagine that your job is the idea you need to express. Now, if you were commiserating with a fellow practitioner (your audience) to achieve sympathy (the outcome you hope to achieve), how would you describe your job in that situation? You'd probably use a lot of jargon and insider language. You'd also be able to talk about some pretty nuanced aspects of what you do. Now imagine instead that you're talking to a six-year-old child (your audience), who's asked what you do out of curiosity (the outcome in this case could be "understanding"). How differently would you describe your job in that situation? I imagine you'd use much simpler language and concepts. The two messages are very different, but your idea—your job—doesn't change.

Your messages are the clothes you put on your "invisible person" of an idea, depending on your audience and the outcome you seek.

This leads me to some more good and bad news. I'll start with the bad: You may have one idea, but you can't ever have just one message about it. There is no such thing as a "one size fits all" version of your message. (Not least because "one size fits all" usually means it doesn't fit anyone well!)

Every time you need your idea to produce a different outcome, it needs to "wear" a different message, just like you need a different outfit depending on whether you want to get in a good workout or have a night out with your friends. Every time your audience changes, or even when the same audience moves closer to acting on your idea, they need a different version of your message—one they can recognize as the answer to a new question in their minds.

Now for the good news. When you build a message about your idea for a particular outcome and audience, two things will happen:

* You'll always find the right version of your idea to put in your message, the Red Thread that's most likely to produce the outcome you want.

* You'll start to understand the true shape of your idea even more, which makes it easier for you to re-dress it for other audiences and other outcomes.

And as you've probably figured out by now, you'll find your Red Thread by defining the audience for your idea and your desired outcome. The easiest way to do that? Decide on the first application of your message. That is, determine where and how you're going to use it.

Step 1: Define an "Application" of Your Message

Defining your message's *application* is generally pretty easy. Simply ask yourself, "Where do I need to talk about my idea?" For the exercises in this book, use the idea you wrote down for the TEDx test in the first chapter.

My client UrSure—a life science/biotech start-up based in Cambridge, Massachusetts—makes simple tests that show doctors whether patients are taking their medications. Since the company is still fairly young, its founders have to talk about their idea all the time, and the stakes are high. They have conversations with potential partners and make pitches to investors. They have a website that those potential stakeholders can go to. They have materials to send ahead or leave behind with doctors and patients. Ultimately, we decided that, to start our work on the Red Thread, the most useful application would be an outline for an initial conversation with potential partners.

There are many other applications you or your business might use.

MARKETING MESSAGES AND MATERIALS:
* Home page copy
* About Us page
* Social media bios
* White paper
* Positioning statement
* Market-level message

STRATEGIC SALES CONVERSATIONS:
* Initial meeting or call
* Conversation or presentation with decision-makers or technical leads
* Final pitch
* Executive summary of a proposal
* Sales deck

PITCHES AND PRESENTATIONS:
* First stage, "about us" presentation
* Investor pitch
* Breakout session

* Keynote presentation
* Multi-part workshop
* Internal conversation asking for commitment or resources

FUNDRAISING ASKS:
* Fundraising materials and slide decks
* Case statements
* First conversation
* The Ask

BOOKS:
* Summary for a book proposal or treatment
* Back cover copy

That's a lot! For now, the trick is to choose just one application to work with. Trust me on this, finding your Red Thread for the first time will be much, much easier if you focus on only one application to start. Once you have the Red Thread for one version of your message, it's much easier to find it for *all* of them.

→ **DO THIS**: Brainstorm all the potential applications of your Red Thread.
Choose the one application to work on first.

Once you know what you're creating, you're ready for the next step.

Step 2: Define the Outcome
Your Message Should Achieve

Recall that your message is the words you need to say to an audience about your idea to achieve a particular *outcome*. Here's how to visualize that: You need to decide what you want your message about that idea to *do*. After all, that's the only way you can know whether or not your message was successful. Did it drive the action you were looking for? We're going to call that action your outcome. The outcome is what you want to happen as a result of your message, both for you and for your audience.

In our work together, UrSure chose a single application, an initial conversation with potential partners, and this outcome: "agree to a demo or trial of the product." With that application and outcome in hand, they knew what the message needed to achieve and could evaluate whether or not it was successful.

→ **DO THIS**: Write down the outcome you want your message to produce with your audience (buy, hire, accept a meeting, support...).

Note: We'll define your audience in the next step. I find people are more likely to know what they want to have happen than to whom they need to talk to make that happen, so I usually recommend starting with outcomes. Sometimes, though, it's easier to start with your audience. The process works either way, so if it feels right for you, feel free to skip ahead and do step 3 first.

THE NARROWER
YOUR FOCUS,
THE BROADER
YOUR REACH.

Step 3: Define the Audience for Your Message

Here's a tip: Your *audience* is *not* "everyone." It can't be. Your idea, and the messages you use to spread that idea, are for people who

* know they have a problem (which your idea solves, whether they know it or not), or

* are actively asking a question (which your idea answers, whether they know it or not).

And I repeat, that's not "everyone."

I get it. With an idea as big and powerful as yours, you want to make sure it reaches as many people as possible. To do that, it helps to understand what author Bill Schley calls the "Universal Paradox of Communication,"[9] which I describe this way: The narrower your focus, the broader your reach.

The Universal Paradox

"Wait, what?" I can hear you say. "If you focus on narrowing your audience (and thus your message), how can you possibly reach more people?"

The simple answer: clarity. Focusing your attention on a single audience, or even a single person, helps you be clearer about what you need to say and how. Think of it this way: Remember the visceral experience of tuning a radio dial to get the station you wanted? Even if you don't, you've probably still had the experience of driving out of range of your favorite radio station, or finally, finally driving back into it... The static. The snippets of sound. Almost hearing it... but not quite. That is not a fun experience. Especially with a super-small physical dial—the tiniest fraction of movement could mean the difference between the annoying *shhh* of... nothing... and the sweet, sweet sounds of the yacht rock. (Okay, maybe not yacht rock for you.)

Then suddenly? *Bam.* There's the music, loud and clear. *Ahhh.*

The station comes through because it broadcasts at only one focused frequency. When you hear it, you've found it. You recognize the station based on the sound.

As with a radio station, you can't "focus" on reach. You can focus only *to* reach. That's why the Universal Paradox is true. If you focus on reach, on trying to aim your message at multiple audiences (or multiple frequencies) at the same time, your message loses strength. No one wants to listen to static. In fact, no one will. They'll tune you and your message out and go looking for something better.

Remember: your message is always, only, and ever the articulation of your idea for *one* audience to achieve *one* outcome.

That's why if you want to broaden your reach, you need to focus your audience.

Focus your audience

The simplest way to identify your audience is simply to apply a *category* to them. The category is who they are or the label you'd put on them. In fact, the category is probably how you currently describe your audience (assuming you've narrowed it down from "everyone," that is). Here are some examples:

* Decision-makers
* Business owners
* Investors
* Parents
* Gamers
* And so on

You can keep it pretty loose, like the categories above, or be more specific by adding some qualifiers. For instance, instead of just "salespeople," you could choose "successful sales leaders," to indicate you're talking to people who manage other salespeople. My client UrSure has multiple audiences. They need investors to invest and medical organizations to partner with to test and deploy their product. They also need doctors to try and then adopt their products. They chose as their application "an initial conversation" that would lead someone to "agree to a demo or trial of the product" (their outcome), so they chose "potential partners in medical organizations."

It can sometimes help to picture a *specific* person your message is for, a real person or an avatar (someone who represents your ideal audience). Often my clients give their ideal audience member a name, because doing so helps them better test their Red Thread against how "Chris" (or "Jordan" or "Dayo") would respond to it.

If your ideal audience member is a real person, obviously you can use their real name. By the way, it's very possible your ideal audience looks a lot like a younger version of yourself, back when you were looking for the answer you've now found! In that case, you can give your audience member *your* name, or some variant of it (for example, "younger Tamsen"). If your audience is an avatar, consider what kind of name makes you think of that person easily. One of my clients chose "Shondra" for her ideal audience, since that brought to mind a group of her friends who she felt would most benefit from her message.

→ **DO THIS**: Write down whom your message is for. Make it both simple and specific. (Don't say "everyone"!)

   If it helps, picture a specific person or kind of person, and give them a name.

"What if I have to talk to one audience about another?"

Sometimes you have to talk to one audience about another audience. For example, whenever UrSure talks to potential partners about their product, they need to explain why and how their product helps another audience: the doctors who ultimately use that product. When UrSure talks to doctors, they need to explain how their product helps yet another audience, the doctors' patients.

   I spent fifteen years working in and for nonprofits, and they deal with this same situation. They often need to ask donors or members for the funds that will support the audience the nonprofit exists to serve: performance-goers, inner-city kids, animals, and so on. You, too, probably deal with these dual-audience situations all the time—like when you have to get your boss's, colleague's, or team member's cooperation to do something, or when you have to go through a gatekeeper to do the real work you do.

It can help to label these two audiences as the "ultimate audience" and the "acting audience." The ultimate audience is those who ultimately benefit from your idea (or product, or service . . . you know the drill). The acting audience is those whose actions you need in order to serve that ultimate audience. UrSure can't make the case for their products to potential partners (the acting audience) without explaining why doctors (the ultimate audience) would want and benefit from it. And in case you're wondering, yes, when UrSure talks directly to doctors, the doctors become the acting audience and their patients become the ultimate audience.

Because of that, the first message you should develop is the one to your *ultimate* audience.

Steps Through the Maze (aka Action Items!)

To finish establishing the context for your Red Thread, have you:

☐ Chosen and noted the first application of your Red Thread?

☐ Written down the outcome you seek for this Red Thread?

☐ Noted the (single!) audience for your message, being as specific as possible?

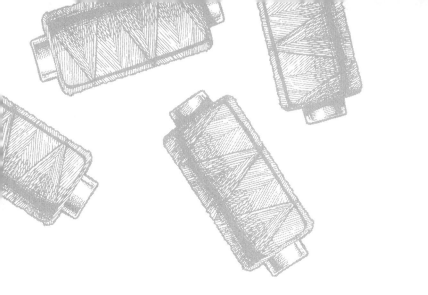

COM

PONENTS

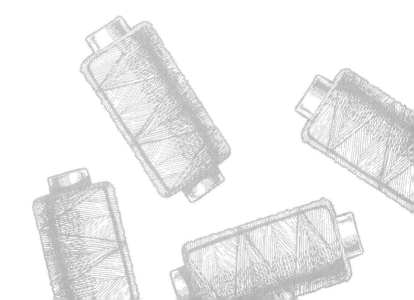

(3)

THE
GOAL

GOAL: Build the story of change people will tell themselves (so you can turn your idea into action, and maybe even change the world).

PROBLEM: For that story to work, it needs to achieve your audience's goals, not just yours.

TRUTH: Your idea is an answer. It's your way of answering a question your audience has about their goal.

CHANGE: Find your audience's question and tie it to your answer.

ACTION: Draft the goal statement of your Red Thread.

AN OPEN
DOOR MAY
TEMPT A SAINT

What Is the Goal Statement?

The *goal statement* component of your message articulates an answer to a question your audience is asking. It should fit comfortably into this sentence:

▌ We can all agree we want to know... [GOAL].

Examples from clients I've worked with look like this: "We can all agree we want to know...

* how we can keep patients on critical medications longer."

* how we can reduce the risk of business decision-making."

* how we can best deliver on our mission."

* how we can feel more comfortable on stage and on camera."

* what incentives will keep millennial employees from leaving."

* how to manage our fear."

* how to get people to perform to their potential."

Here's another one: "how we can best symbolize our commitment to each other." It's not from a client of mine, but it is one of my favorite examples of how our brains create a story to justify a decision—and of how a company can create the story you end up telling yourself about it. It's also an example that may be sitting on the finger of someone you know... or on your own.

What is it? A diamond engagement ring.

Back in the early 1930s, De Beers, the diamond company, had a worldwide monopoly on diamonds (they still do). I hate to break it to you, but diamonds, in and of themselves, don't have a lot of intrinsic value. Their value in the marketplace—and the premium price we pay in the retail market—comes from two sources. First, as the worldwide monopoly holder, De Beers can control the number of (mined) diamonds in the marketplace. That limits the supply and as a result drives up the price. In the earlier part of the last century, De Beers had pretty much maxed out the industrial demand for diamonds, so they set their sights on a new outcome and a new audience: sell more diamonds to the retail market.

But in the 1930s, diamonds didn't mean much to the average person on the street. They weren't the standard, solitary stone for an engagement ring. Even though diamonds on engagement rings date back to the fifteenth century, in the early part of the twentieth century, they were often just one of a variety of stones jewelers used. Indeed, for the average engaged couple, engagement rings often weren't part of the picture at

all. When they were looking for something to symbolize the commitment they had for each other, couples
often focused on the ring itself as the symbol: something with no beginning and no end.

De Beers wanted to know: How could they get more
people to shift their focus to the *kind* of ring couples
exchanged? And how could they do so in such a way
that average people would buy something previously
reserved for only the very wealthy? De Beers made not
just the ring but the stone—the diamond—a symbol.
And they did it with four words: "A diamond is forever,"
the tagline they introduced in (get this!) 1947.

But ... how? This brings in the second source of
diamonds' value and price: the story you tell yourself
about what diamonds *mean*. With that four-word tagline, De Beers took the previous story in people's minds
about engagement rings—any unbroken circle would
do—and replaced it with another one: "The best way
to symbolize our commitment to each other is with a
diamond ring."

I'll continue to build on this example throughout
the book, but note that the story of diamond rings
started, as all great stories do, when De Beers learned
what their audience wanted. De Beers wanted to sell
more diamond rings—that was their desired outcome.
Engaged couples wanted the best symbol of their
commitment—that's the goal.

When you know what someone wants, you know
where the story starts.

So, that's where the story began.

GOAL STATEMENT CRITERIA

1. A goal statement needs to express a goal your audience wants to achieve, a problem they want to solve, or a need they want to meet.

2. It needs to be in your audience's language, not yours. That means no jargon or trademarked phrases your audience wouldn't use.

How to Build Your Goal Statement

With your outcome in hand, you know what your message needs to do for you. But to build a story people will tell themselves, you also need to know how your idea achieves something *for your audience*. In fact, the story doesn't begin until it helps them get something they want.

Your idea is an answer to a question your audience is asking. So, you need to identify that question, which will, in effect, tie your answer to what your audience wants. We're going to use your audience's question to draft the goal statement of your Red Thread.

Define the audience's question

To define your audience's question—one your audience would ask, out loud, to their friends and colleagues—you've got to determine what they are actively asking right now. What is the pain point that's driving them to look for a solution?

You're ultimately trying to find a goal statement for which, if you asked them, "Would you agree you want this?" they'd answer "yes," without hesitation. People don't readily *un*want something they want. So, the more you anchor your message in a question they're actively trying to answer, the more they'll want to hear your message. Perhaps even better, their brains will recognize the start of a story—establishing a goal!

Sometimes the whole reason you're building a Red Thread is that your audience—and maybe even the world—is asking the "wrong" question, at least to your point of view. "I know everyone wants to know x," you say, "but what they *really* should be asking is y." You may think I'm nuts here, but the question you want is that first, "wrong" one. (Hold on to the second, "right" one though; it has a role to play later in your Red Thread!) Why is the "wrong" question right? *Because that's what your audience wants right now.* That's what they're looking for and what they'll pay attention to.

Discovering your audience's question almost always makes your goal statement clearer and shorter. It also helps you keep your goal statement in the language of your audience.

→ **DO THIS**: Brainstorm questions your audience is asking right now, even the "wrong" ones. Make sure your idea can answer those questions for your audience. Most critically, make sure your audience would ask those questions (or ones close to them) out loud, to friends and colleagues.

Choose a question you can realistically answer in the time and space you have for your message.

At this point, you may be asking, "How can I be sure this is the *right* audience question?" The answer depends on three things: your prior knowledge of your audience, your time frame for developing your message, and your tolerance for risk. Many of my clients already have a deep knowledge of their audience and what they want and need right now. Sometimes that comes through experience; sometimes it comes through more formal research. If you don't have that deep knowledge already, you can get it from a number of different places:

- Examine the search strings that bring people to your website (if you have one).

- See what kinds of questions or search strings about your topic autofill in search engines. (Type a keyword or the start of a question and see what the search engine suggests.)

- Go to search aggregators like answerthepublic.com to see what questions people most often ask about a particular topic or keyword.

- Talk to your customer-facing staff, if you have them— customer service representatives, salespeople, and so on—and find out what people ask them.

- Engage in more formal forms of research, like focus groups or studies.

- Try to remember what question you asked when you first started exploring your idea. By remembering where you or your organization started, you can find the logical starting place for someone who doesn't know what you do and work from there.

* Look at your original intake forms or notes for your clients and customers—what did they say the problem was then? (*Pro tip:* If you don't have that question on your intake forms now, add it!)

* You can also simply choose the question you *want* to answer—all that takes is your imagination!

The one thing to avoid? Asking your current clients *now* why they came to you. After working with you or your idea, your clients will suffer from the "curse of knowledge" I mentioned earlier. They know what they've actually achieved through your idea now, but they usually forget what they were looking for when they started.

If you're confident in your question, feel free to move to the next chapter. Sometimes, though, your audience's question isn't immediately clear. If that's the case, spend some more time getting into your audience's mindset. How? By figuring out what they want, value, and struggle with.

What do they want, value, and struggle with?

Even if you readily come up with the question your audience is asking, it's useful to understand their current perspective—the lens through which they will view your message. When you can see the world as your audience sees it, you can more easily grasp why they'd be interested in your message, or even better, be convinced your idea is the right answer for them. I've found that assessing what your audience wants, values, and struggles with helps define that perspective clearly. Let's look at each of these elements more closely.

Defining *what they want* means identifying a high-level outcome they're looking for right now. It provides context for your audience's specific goal and often reveals the underlying motivation for it. Typically, these are the kinds of things that can help your audience make, save, or improve their financial situation, their job, their sanity, or their life. Frame the want in positive terms your audience would realistically use themselves when talking with someone else. This is not what you *think* they want. It's what they *say* they want. For instance:

- "How can we improve patient outcomes?"
- "How can we improve profitability?"
- "How can we keep our community engaged and informed?"
- "How can I raise awareness of me and my company?"
- "How can we better retain our millennial employees?"
- "How can I be who I *really* want to be?"
- "How can we drive more sales?"

You also want to *identify a value* your audience shares with you. In fact, they must have this value to be open to your idea and message, even if it's not what's driving their want. Why? Because people won't agree with anything at odds with their fundamental values (at least not long-term). For example, another of my clients is a manufacturer of premium devices used in scientific research. Their audience is "research scientists" who want to publish the successful results of their work. The audience must share the value of "credibility" with my client, or else they wouldn't be willing to pay the premium prices for my client's products. (They could go with a less expensive option for a particular piece of equipment, but they wouldn't be able to rely on the results as confidently.)

Your audience doesn't necessarily have to say they have this value, but it needs to be one they would easily agree with. Here are some examples of values to help you get started:

* Innovation/creativity/trying something new
* Continuous improvement/self-improvement/curiosity/continuous learning
* Accuracy/reliability
* Fiscal responsibility
* The power of face-to-face communication
* Work-life balance/people-first approach to management

The final component of your audience's perspective is *what they struggle with*, in relation to what they want and what they value. Think of this as a pain point that could drive them to action. Sometimes this is a more focused take on their want, like, "*What specific steps can I take* to improve my quality of life while living with this disease?" "*How can I build my confidence* so I can have a voice at the table?" Sometimes the struggle arises from conflict or tension between the want and value: "How can we improve productivity *while still caring* for our people?" Like the want, the struggle needs to be something your audience would realistically say when talking with someone else. Here are some additional examples:

- "How can we keep patients on critical medications longer?"

- "How can we best use Big Data to reduce risk in our decision-making?"

- "What's the best way to engage with new audiences while still serving our core audiences?"

- "How can I become more comfortable on stage and on camera?"

- "What loyalty incentives are millennial employees more likely to respond to?"

- "How can I manage my fear?"

- "How can I get people to perform to their potential?"

You might be wondering why the want and the struggle have to be something the audience would realistically say to someone else. Using the audience's language helps ensure your audience perceives your message as relevant to them, without any convincing from you. When your audience sees your message as relevant, they are much more likely to pay attention to it and to you. Paying attention is the first step to action.

And don't worry: you will eventually get to reveal how your message gives your audience what they *really* want and need... just not yet. Keep all your brainstorms, though—they'll come in handy in the last piece of your Red Thread, when you revisit this original goal in chapter 8.

Once you have all the elements of your audience identified, you can summarize them with an audience statement that fills in these blanks:

This message is for [CATEGORY] who [WANT], value [VALUE], but struggle with [STRUGGLE].

Filling that in will give you a statement like this: "This message is for...

* patients and providers who want to improve patient outcomes, value innovation, but struggle with how to keep patients on critical medications longer."

* business decision-makers who want to improve profitability, value accuracy and reliability, but struggle with how best to use Big Data to reduce risk."

* the executive team, who wants to keep the community engaged and informed, values fiscal responsibility, but struggles with how to engage with new audiences while still serving our core audiences."

* entrepreneurs who want to raise awareness of their thought leadership and company, value the power of face-to-face communication, but struggle with feeling comfortable on stage and on camera."

* senior company leaders who want to retain their millennial employees better, value a people-first

approach to management, but struggle with figuring out what loyalty incentives millennial employees will respond to."

* goal-oriented leaders who want the freedom to be who they really want to be, value self-improvement, but struggle with how to manage their fear."

* current and future sales leaders who want to drive more sales, value others' success as a path to their own, but struggle with how to get their team members to perform to their potential."

Once you have those components, use them to clarify your audience question even further. Their want or struggle becomes the heart of the goal statement.

→ **DO THIS**: Brainstorm your audience's wants, values, and struggles. (Keep all your brainstorms, even the ones you don't use now—you may want to use them again later.)

Fill in the blanks of your audience statement.

Draw your goal statement from your audience's specific want or struggle.

When doing this want/value/struggle exercise, you'll sometimes find that those three elements can "move around." A struggle can be a want, a want can be a value, and so on. Choosing what belongs where is a big part of clarifying the message. Even then, though, it may not be clear which audience question is the "right" one to get the outcome you want from this application. When that happens, go one step further and figure out the more universal needs that may be driving their question.

WHEN YOU KNOW
WHAT SOMEONE WANTS,
YOU KNOW WHERE
THE STORY STARTS.

Maslow's Hierarchy of Needs

When writing a goal statement that applies to the largest possible audience, it can sometimes help to look at audience needs that are universal. While psychologist Abraham Maslow's Hierarchy of Needs has its fans and detractors, it at least offers a framework for thinking through the different kinds of needs your audience may be experiencing.

Maslow's hierarchy is usually shown visually, as a triangle or a pyramid. At the wide base are the needs for basic physiological survival, things like food, water, warmth, and rest. Next come "safety" needs: secure resources, employment, health, family, and so on. Those are followed by needs for love and belonging and then by "esteem," both of self and by others. Needs related to purpose, fulfillment, creativity, and the like are all part of "self-actualization" at the top of the pyramid.

Those universal needs apply when you're talking to individuals, but what about companies? I developed a *business* version of Maslow's hierarchy (figure 1), which you can use to think through potential goal statements, as well.

The questions from the bottom of the pyramid relate to what's necessary for business survival. I put questions about determining basic offerings—having something to sell—and earning capital into that category:

- "How can we make more money, because it's necessary for survival?"
- "How can we get more customers?"
- "How do we find customers?"

Figure 1: The Hierarchy of Business Needs

Moving up this business hierarchy, safety and security questions often show up as questions about systems and processes. At that level, your audience questions might be things like: "How can we make sure we retain our customers?" That's a slightly higher-level question because your audience isn't in survival mode. They already have clients and a secure foundation: you can only retain customers if you already have them.

Above questions about systems and processes likely come questions about culture and employee engagement (the equivalent of love and belonging), then awards and recognition (esteem), and then finally about market and industry leadership (self-actualization).

→ **DO THIS**: Brainstorm a list of audience questions for each level of the pyramid and then turn them into goal statements.

Choose the goal statement that best serves your needs and your audience's.

Note: You will capture fewer people with a goal from higher up the hierarchy. It's a triangle for a reason; more people are at the bottom than at the top. When in doubt, go as low on the hierarchy as you reasonably can.

Save Your Work!

You'll notice I've been encouraging you to save your work. Throughout this process, it's useful to keep all your brainstorms. Why? It comes back to the Agatha Christie quote that started this book: "Words... are only the outer clothing of ideas." It's kind of like the paper dolls I grew up with or, these days, the skins on Minecraft avatars. You're putting different outfits or covers on the same basic form.

When it comes to the goal statement, various people are going to ask different versions of what is, essentially, the same question. Those differences will be based on who they are, how ready they are to act, how likely they are to agree with your answer, and where they'll see or hear your answer. Having all the variations helps you do (at least) three things:

* Recognize a wider variety of potential clients or customers, because you'll have identified all the questions your idea can ultimately answer.

* Reach a wider variety of potential clients and customers, because you'll be able to frame your idea through all those different starting points.

* Start to see the path from one question to another— as people move up to the hierarchy of needs or gain knowledge or readiness—that can help you plan a series of messages.

No matter how many goal statements you brainstorm, remember to pick one to start and make sure it answers a question your audience would actually ask. That's the only way to get the clarity you and your audience need for your message to succeed.

When in doubt, go back to your work on your application, outcome, and audience. Which of the questions and goal statements you've brainstormed can you address successfully in your application to achieve the outcome you want with that audience? Go with that one. (And don't worry, you can always go back and change it!)

Starting the Journey

Your message is a map from where your audience is now to your idea. It retraces the steps of the story you told yourself about your idea, in the language, wants, and beliefs of your audience. The goal statement starts the story your audience will tell themselves about your idea ("This will help me get what I want... so I'm going to see where it goes") and captures their starting point. Once you have your audience's question framed in their own language, you're ready to move on to the next step: creating the conditions that will help them take the first step toward your answer. But that presents, literally, a problem.

Steps Through the Maze (aka Action Items!)

To find the goal statement of your Red Thread, have you:

☐ Listed the questions your chosen audience is asking right now?

☐ Chosen the question that best serves your needs and your audience's and turned it into a goal statement?

☐ If you're struggling, brainstormed your audience's wants, values, and struggles and put together an audience statement, and/or used the Hierarchy of Business Needs to test how your idea could answer questions at each level?

(4)

THE
PROBLEM

GOAL: Build the story of change people will tell themselves (so you can turn your idea into action, and maybe even change the world).

PROBLEM: When making the case for our ideas, we often focus more on what the audience is doing than on what they're seeing.

TRUTH: How we see drives what we do. The best predictor of behavior is our beliefs about ourselves and the world—beliefs that don't change quickly.

CHANGE: Find the "problem" in your audience's perspective—a new, contrasting way of seeing the world that's consistent with their current beliefs.

ACTION: Draft the problem statement of your Red Thread.

IT TAKES TWO
TO HAVE AN
ARGUMENT

What Is the Problem Statement?

Fundamentally, your *problem statement* explains the real reason your audience has been struggling to achieve their goal. It follows your goal statement (We can all agree we want to know... [GOAL]), and should fit comfortably in this sentence:

> Despite the barriers we all know exist, the real problem is... [TWO-PART PROBLEM].

In the list of some of my clients' problem statements below, notice the pairs of words that suggest the two-part nature of the problem: "Despite the barriers we all know exist, the real problem is...

* having to rely more on what patients *recall* than on what tests *reveal*."

* Big Data doesn't just create *more knowledge*, it creates *more unknowns*."

* the relationship between '*content output*' (how much we produce) and '*content exposure*' (who sees it, and how many)."

* seeing fear as *one big thing*, rather than as *a collection of many things*."

- focusing on *positions* more than on the *people* in them."

- we think the answer lies more in *being fearless* than in *fearing fear itself less*."

- we hope for *leaders* while training *followers*, however unintentionally."

To show how the problem statement builds on the goal statement, let's return to the De Beers example again. The audience is engaged couples. If back in 1947 De Beers had been writing a goal statement, it would have needed to incorporate a question those couples were reasonably asking, let's say, "What's the best symbol of our commitment to each other?" The problem statement would have needed to introduce how couples try to answer that question: by seeing a ring as the symbol. The problem statement would also have needed to include the new perspective De Beers wanted to introduce: focusing on the *kind* of ring. Putting the goal statement and the problem statement together, De Beers' Red Thread might have read:

> We can all agree we want to know the best symbol of our commitment we can give to each other. Despite the barriers we all know exist, the real problem is a *ring* is a symbol, but the *kind of ring* can be a symbol, too.

PROBLEM STATEMENT CRITERIA

1. The problem statement should be something the audience is not already consciously aware of.

2. They should be able to do something about it (for example, "fear" is not something the audience can address directly).

3. It should always have two parts—something that represents their current perspective, and something that represents yours.

4. It can be summarized in a "problem pair"—a pair of words or short phrases that complement each other and/or have a relationship that the audience would readily acknowledge and understand.

5. Both parts are required for the change or solution you recommend but are not the solution itself.

The Problem with Problems

In crafting your goal statement, you found the audience question that your idea answers. You also started the story of your idea by establishing something your audience wants and is unlikely to stop wanting. But if your audience wants that answer so badly, why haven't they found it yet? Your problem statement will describe why.

Remember that the second step of story structure is to introduce a problem someone didn't know they had. In stories, this previously unknown obstacle creates conflict and tension, which is the engine of action. For your message to successfully drive your audience to action, you, too, need to introduce a problem your audience doesn't yet know they have.

More often than not, the true underlying problem, or barrier to your audience's goal, is how they see the situation or themselves. It's a "problem" of perspective that, as long as it exists, means they can't "see" the path to their goal. How your audience views the world drives their actions. So, to change what people *do*, you need to change how they *see*.

Simple, right? Eh . . . not quite.

Here's why: how people view the world is rooted in their beliefs. And beliefs aren't easy to change. In fact, when you challenge someone's beliefs, they're much more likely to dig in and believe them more—and that's usually fatal to your idea. So, how do we solve this "problem with the problem"? By introducing a new, contrasting perspective (yours!) that's still consistent with your audience's current beliefs. De Beers didn't try to get people to buy a necklace instead of a ring. They validated the current answer (rings) and introduced a variant of that answer that was comfortable to the audience (kinds of rings). That combination of "current" and "contrasting but consistent" perspectives is the two-part "problem pair" that you'll turn into your problem statement.

But that's *telling* you what the problem statement is supposed to do. Now let me show you, too.

Meet the "Duck Bunny"

Take a look at the illustration in figure 2, an optical illusion from 1892. If you look closely, you can see two different animals. (*Hint:* They're in the title to this section).

Welche Thiere gleichen einander am meisten?

Kaninchen und Ente.

Figure 2: Which two animals are most alike?
Source: *Fliegende Blätter*, October 23, 1892, Wikimedia Commons.

What did you see? If you can read German, the answer may have been even clearer, since the words translate to, "Which two animals are most alike? Rabbit and duck." This "Duck Bunny," as I like to call it, is my favorite way to help you think about the two parts of your problem statement and how they relate to each other. Why? Because it illustrates what psychologists call "reframing." Let me explain.

Based on my very unscientific survey, most people see the duck first. (Yes, even when I don't call it the Duck Bunny ahead of time!) For simplicity's sake, then, think of the duck as representing your audience's current perspective. If you didn't see it before, now look for the bunny (the duck's beak turns into the bunny's ears). Think of the bunny as representing the contrasting yet consistent perspective you want to introduce.

No matter which animal you see first, though, both are "right." The challenge for both you and your audience? *You can't see one if you're focused on the other.* Reframing is getting someone who's focused on the duck to see the bunny instead.

That's exactly what your problem statement needs to do. It needs to introduce both the duck and the bunny—the current and new perspectives—to start the process of your audience focusing in a new direction.

How to Build Your Problem Statement

Now that you've met the Duck Bunny, the simplest way to describe how to build your problem statement is this: find the Duck, find the Bunny, then put them together into your problem statement. Sometimes that's as easy as listening to yourself as you describe what you see as the "real" problem standing in the way of your audience's goal. Anytime you catch yourself saying something like "People think the problem is x, but it's really y" or "I wonder if we focused over here rather than over there..." *pay attention*! Anytime you set up a "Duck versus Bunny" contrast like that, it's possible your story-based brain has just delivered your problem statement to you.

Other times, though, you need to shine a bit more light on the maze of your mind. In that case, like Theseus, take it step by step.

Step 1: Find the Duck—your audience's current way of seeing barriers to their goal

The reason you see a duck in the Duck Bunny comes down to how your brain interprets the set of individual lines that make up the drawing. Those lines are like the barriers your audience sees as getting in the way of their goal.

When you can (1) find those known barriers and (2) determine what they have in common, you can (3) show your audience that the barriers they know about are actually part of a larger picture.

For example, one of my clients, a leadership and culture consulting practice called PROPEL, works with CEOs and high-level HR managers on issues of employee engagement and company culture. In our work together, the founders, Jamie Notter and Maddie Grant, chose the question, "How can I get more energy and commitment out of my people?" as the audience goal. As we worked to find the problem statement, Jamie and Maddie started listing the barriers to *most* people's goals: time, money, and other people. (*Pro tip:* If you're ever struggling to figure out the known barriers, you can start with "time, money, and other people," too!) They then dug a little deeper to discover what those barriers had in common. They noticed that when talking about the time, their clients would say things like, "Our people are already working fifty-plus hours a week... and aren't happy about it!" The money barrier often showed up as, "No matter how much we pay people, they're still not happy, and we're not getting results!" And while this wasn't usually the case with Jamie and Maddie's clients, if the barrier of "other people" appeared, it was in a complaint like, "There's no way to make them happy; they're just not happy people."

Do you see what Jamie and Maddie started to see? The word "happy" kept popping up. They realized their clients saw the barriers to their goal of more employee engagement in terms of *happiness*. Leaders and HR executives were seeing "energy and commitment" and "employee happiness" as one and the same. "Happiness" was the Duck!

→ **DO THIS**: List the barriers your audience sees as getting in the way of their goal.

Determine what those barriers have in common.

Frame those commonalities in terms of a single concept.

In addition to considering time, money, and other people as barriers in your audience's perspective, you can also look back over the "struggles" you came up with when writing your goal statement. What patterns do you see? Why does your audience think those are barriers? What language do they use to describe those barriers?

In the beginning, thinking in categories like this may feel difficult. Rest assured, though, that the difficulty is only because consciously thinking this way is unfamiliar. It is, however, far from unnatural. In fact, as psychologist Susan Weinschenk notes, "people naturally create categories. Just as learning a native language happens naturally, so does learning to categorize the world around us."[10] We're able to create categories from as young as age seven, because we must in order to make sense of the world.

And ultimately, that's what you're doing for your audiences when you help them understand the problem of perspective that's getting in their way. You're helping them make sense of the barriers they see in front of them (Duck!), just in time to give them a *new* perspective (Bunny!) that opens a new path to their goal.

Step 2: Find the Bunny—a new way for your audience to see their current situation

Once you have some ideas about your Duck, it's time to start finding your Bunny—a different picture produced by the same lines. More specifically, you're looking for a different way for your audience to look at the Duck barriers. Just like the Duck Bunny illustration itself, you're not introducing new information here, just a new *interpretation* of what they're already experiencing.

If we go back to PROPEL, Jamie and Maddie knew the Duck was likely happiness, but what was the Bunny? Remember, their audiences equated the goal of "more energy and commitment" with more employee happiness. Based on their research, however, Jamie and Maddie knew there was another way to look at what drove employee engagement. What they found was that employee *happiness* (the Duck) was a side effect of something else: feelings of *success* (the Bunny). In other words, employees' success drives their energy and commitment. Happiness often just comes along for the ride.

With that discovery, Maddie and Jamie could reframe their audience's known barriers through that new lens. People's frustrations with their work hours (time) were because they weren't seeing the successful effects of all those hours, either for themselves or for the company... so of course they weren't happy. Same with salaries—as the old saying goes, "money doesn't buy happiness." If people didn't feel successful at work (something measured by far more than salary), no amount of money would make up for that. Even the "other people" barrier looked quite different through the new lens of success: Jamie and Maddie found that even unhappy people can be engaged... if they feel successful.

I need to stress: *the current client focus on happiness wasn't "wrong."* Happiness *is* part of the employee engagement equation, just like the Duck *is* part of the Duck Bunny illusion. But when Jamie and Maddie showed their clients that success *also* explained the barriers in front of them, their ultimate solution—"solve for success"—became a way for their clients to get both the engagement and the happiness they were looking for... not to mention a much more successful company. Ultimately, that realization turned into this problem statement: "Despite the barriers we all know exist, the real problem is seeing 'engagement' and 'happiness' as interchangeable rather than inter*related*."

→ **DO THIS**: Starting with the concept that represents your audience's current perspective on their known barriers (the Duck), brainstorm contrasting concepts that represent your perspective (the Bunny).

Once you have some ideas about both parts of your Duck Bunny—the "now" and "new" perspectives—it's time to put them together.

Step 3: Turn your two-part problem (aka Duck Bunny) into your problem statement

Including both parts of your Duck Bunny in your problem statement does something crucial: it provides contrast. That's important, because we humans need contrast to see—both literally and metaphorically. In human vision, contrast allows us to distinguish one object from another. Imagine, for example, how hard it would be to navigate an all-black room, with all-black furniture and fixtures, all with no light! Light provides the contrast that lets you see where a chair stops and a table begins. Without that contrast... ouch! You'll inevitably walk into something.

In human cognition and perception, contrast serves a similar purpose. You may understand what a dog is, but you understand it even better when you contrast it with a cat. By seeing the differences between the two, in fact, you understand both the dog and the cat better. That's why you want to present your audience with a problem statement that has two parts—Duck *and* Bunny. It helps your audience not only "see" how their current perspective is different from yours, but also understand both parts better, individually.

In fact, finding a pair of concepts that work as a Duck Bunny helps *you* understand the problem better! That's why, in this third step, your goal is to find two concepts that work to describe each individual perspective well, and that work together.

→ **DO THIS**: Combine your step 1 and step 2 concepts into your problem pair (Duck Bunny), a pair of words or short phrases that are related but in tension with each other.

One way to do this is to play with your pair of concepts to make them work together well in people's ears. There's a word that we can borrow from poetry for this: "prosody." (Such a good word!) We can also borrow some techniques from poetry:

* Alliteration—repeated words that begin with the same letter, as in "assess, articulate, activate"

* Assonance—repeated words that have similar *interior* sounds, as in "try, find, fight"

* Rhyme—"know, go, flow"

* Number or pattern of syllables—"inspiration, activation"

One of my favorite tools for this process is an alliteration synonym finder. There are several online, but I use the one at alliteration.me the most.

Working on the prosody of your problem pair often helps you find them in the first place. It also opens up your line of thinking to words and concepts you otherwise wouldn't have thought of. Using "interchangeable" to describe Maddie and Jamie's audience perspective, for instance, led us to "interrelated" as a way to sum up the new perspective Maddie and Jamie wanted to present. Both words start similarly (alliteration) and have the same number of syllables.

One more benefit: because the human brain loves patterns and connections like those prosody can provide, having a prosodic problem pair can make it easier for both you and your audience to remember.

→ **DO THIS**: Refine the problem pair with the alliteration, assonance, rhyming, and patterns of poetry (prosody).

Draft a problem statement that includes both parts of your problem pair.

If you're looking for inspiration for your own problem pair, review the list of problem statements at the beginning of the chapter and the De Beers example.

TO CHANGE

WHAT PEOPLE *DO*,

YOU NEED TO CHANGE

HOW THEY *SEE*.

If You Get Stuck

Find the problem pair with metaphors

To jump-start your thinking on what the problem pair might be for your message, think of some well-known Duck Bunnies:

* Forest/trees—as in, "You can't see the forest for the trees." Is someone so focused on the details, they can't see the big picture? Or so focused on the big picture, they can't see what's creating it?

* Cart/horse—as in, "Putting the cart before the horse." Is someone seeing the right components, but in reverse order?

* Right hand/left hand—as in, "The right hand doesn't know what the left hand is doing." Is someone so focused on one part of an equation that the whole is out of balance?

* Shallow/deep—Is someone only looking at the surface and missing the deeper implications? Or vice versa?

* Centralized/decentralized, parts/whole, hub/spoke, pieces/process, show/tell, me/you, known/unknown ... you get the idea ...

Once you have a general type of problem pair, customize the words and language to fit your audience's situation and the words they're familiar with or would use themselves. In one of the examples I listed at the beginning of the chapter, my client customized the problem pair known/unknown to become "more knowledge/more unknowns." Together, we turned it into this problem statement: "Big Data doesn't just create more knowledge, it creates more unknowns."

Find the problem by "going to the library"

I recently discovered one specific metaphor that can help you find your problem pair: a library. Since your audience is asking a question, imagine they go to a library to find their answer. What section do they go to first to find their answer? What section *should* they go to?

One of my clients, for instance, said her audience was trying to find an answer on dealing with crises in the "communications" section. In her mind, though, the real answer lay in a section on "nature." Instead of looking for *scripts*, her clients should look for *systems* that prevent crises in the first place.

Find the problem pair using variables (math style!)

Sometimes you can find the problem pair by playing with how your perspective and your audience's relate to each other. Since those are both "unknowns" for you, treat it like a math problem and use variables like x and y as placeholders. I typically use x for the audience's current perspective (Duck) and y for the new, contrasting perspective (Bunny), asking questions like these:

* Do people think x and y are the same thing? (For example, the problem pair ring/kind of ring becomes the problem statement "a ring is a symbol, but the kind of ring can be a symbol, too.")

* Do people miss that y follows x, or vice versa? (The problem pair doing/seeing becomes: "we often focus more on what the audience is doing than on what they're seeing.")

* Is x really just a subset of y, or vice versa? (The problem pair one thing/one thing made of many things becomes: "seeing fear as one big thing, rather than as a collection of many things.")

Once you've figured out the relationship between x and y, build your problem statement.

→ **DO THIS**: Using the variables x and y, determine the relationship between your audience's current perspective (x) and your new (contrasting, consistent) one (y).

Draft a problem statement that includes both variables of your problem pair.

Why the Problem Isn't Fear

One of the criteria at the opening of this chapter was that the problem couldn't be "fear." There are three reasons why. First, fear is a feeling. It is an *effect* of a fear-inducing situation. It can also be a driver of certain behaviors. But we humans can't stop the fear itself.

We can only stop what causes fear or what it causes us to do. Don't present your audience with an unsolvable problem or an impossible change—that's the opposite of helping them achieve their goal! Unfortunately, telling your audience "don't be afraid" is exactly that: an impossible change. The fear will come unless your audience changes the situation that creates it. The fear will have its negative effects until your audience changes their reactions to it.

The second reason I'm taking fear off the table as a problem is that it's usually not an unknown. Although some people may truly not realize that fear is holding them back, I've found that many people do—even if they don't admit it easily or publicly. But remember, if it's a known problem, then it's likely a candidate for being in your goal statement. (For example, "How can I feel confident in making x change?")

Finally, remember that the problem must have two parts that you bring together. If you can turn fear into something with two parts, great. More commonly, though, to create two parts, you need to focus on what causes the fear or on what that fear is making the audience do or not do. The two parts have to complete the picture. Fear alone can't do that.

Frame It and Name It

Your first several attempts at a problem statement will probably be pretty wordy. That's okay. Keep working until you can distill the statement to its core words or phrases. That's when you know you have enough clarity to share the real problem with your audience. I often tell my clients they can (and probably should) have at least two versions of their problem statement:

* A "fast version," which is the summary in a problem pair, such as doing/seeing.

* A "full version," which incorporates all the detail necessary to fully understand the two different perspectives.

The full version allows you to frame the problem in detail for your audience so they understand it. Then, with the fast version, you give them an easy way to remember and repeat the problem to others. Sometimes a problem statement allows you to go one step further and assign a name to the problem itself. When I was working with my client Jacob Engel, a leadership coach and consultant for business owners, he came up with a fantastic name for the problem he had framed.

Jacob had identified his audience question as, "How can I hire and retain the best talent?" The problem as he saw it was, "even though there are many voices at the table, only one tends to matter—the leader's," which he could summarize as "many voices/one voice." From Jacob's experience, he knew that when people didn't feel heard at their jobs, they tended to leave.

Jacob wanted to make sure his message was differentiated, however, so I suggested he name the problem to claim some ownership of the point of view. That's when he asked if I ever watched *Britain's Got Talent*. (I didn't.) Jacob explained that one of the recent winners was a comic known as the "Lost Voice Guy." The contestant called himself that because, due to a disability, he couldn't speak—a computer delivered all his jokes for him. Jacob saw a connection between the Lost Voice Guy and the problem he was trying to name: the non-leader voices were getting lost, and thus, Jacob's "Lost Voice Problem" was born.

→ **DO THIS**: Once you've defined your problem pair and drafted your problem statement, look for opportunities to give your problem a name.

Make the Problem Impossible to Ignore

Even if your problem statement is beautifully crafted, summarized, and even named, your message is still not quite ready to do its work in the world. It's not even ready for your solution. No, if you really want to change how people see—and change what they do—you first have to make the problem impossible to ignore. To do that, you'll need to find the truth.

Steps Through the Maze (aka Action Items!)

To find the two-part problem statement of your Red Thread, have you:

- [ ] Described your audience's current view of the barriers they see as getting in the way of their goal (i.e., have you found the Duck)?

- [ ] Described your contrasting view of those same barriers (the Bunny)?

- [ ] Worked with both of those sets to find a crisp, concise problem pair (the Duck Bunny)?

- [ ] Turned those two short words or phrases into a two-part problem statement?

- [ ] Used prosody, metaphor, and x/y variables to work through struggles creating your problem statement?

- [ ] Should it be useful to you, given your problem a name you can own?

(5)

THE TRUTH

GOAL: Build the story of change people will tell themselves (so you can turn your idea into action, and maybe even change the world).

PROBLEM: You can't create change in someone else, only the conditions for it. Change comes from choice; choice comes from conflict.

TRUTH: I often tell people, when two truths fight, only one lives. When two things we want or believe to be true are in conflict with each other, we will always choose the one closest to our true goals.

CHANGE: Engineer a moment of truth: create an internal conflict for your audience that makes inaction impossible.

ACTION: Draft the truth statement of your Red Thread.

YOU CAN ONLY LEAN AGAINST SOMETHING STRONG

What Is the Truth Statement?

The *truth statement* describes something that creates an internal conflict in the minds of your audience. It follows your problem statement (Despite the barriers we all know exist, the real problem is... [TWO-PART PROBLEM]) and should fit comfortably in this sentence:

❚ Yet we can agree it's true that... [TRUTH].

Some examples look like this: "Yet we can agree it's true that...

* seeing is believing."

* the greatest risk comes from the unknown."

* the more people who see our content, the more impact it will have."

* experiences leave imprints—fear leaves physical traces in our bodies."

* people are what make positions work."

* you're an everyday improviser—every day you have to figure out how to handle something you didn't plan for."

* leadership is learned."

I often tell audiences and my clients that the De Beers tagline of "a diamond is forever" is the best truth statement that everyone already knows. While engineers often disagree with me on this, most of us already know that diamonds are (1) very hard and (2) very hard to destroy, at least in ordinary circumstances. So, most people would agree, then, that a diamond literally is "forever," or close to it.

When that literal "truth" is put in the context of the goal and problem, something magical takes place—the literal turns metaphorical. Read the hypothetical De Beers Red Thread so far:

> We can all agree we want to know the best symbol of our commitment we can give to each other. Despite the barriers we all know exist, the real problem is a ring is a symbol, but the kind of ring can be a symbol, too. Yet we can agree it's true that a diamond is forever...

Do you see what happens? In the context of symbols and rings, the literal "foreverness" of a diamond becomes symbolic. It doesn't take away from the symbol of the ring, it adds to it. But that creates a new conflict for the audience. Suddenly something they believe ("a diamond is forever—literally") puts what they want (the "best symbol") in jeopardy—and all because they haven't been paying attention to the *kind* of ring. Uh-oh.

That conflict creates what's known as a "moment of truth."

TRUTH STATEMENT CRITERIA

1. The truth statement needs to be a self-evident value, belief, fact, or discovery that your audience would easily agree with.

2. To help with that, it needs to be something your audience can validate without you (through their own experience or via a third party, like published and/or peer-reviewed research).

3. It should be something that already exists in your audience's belief ecosystem or readily could.

4. It must explain why the problem is such a problem, in a way that makes the problem impossible to ignore.

5. It must explain why the change you're going to introduce is the only one that makes sense.

6. It contains no "prescriptive" or directive language; it simply describes the way things are.

7. Ideally, it is a neutral statement that could be interpreted both negatively and positively.

Making Inaction Impossible

All great stories have a moment of truth. Sometimes it's called the "climax," sometimes it's called the "point of no return." If you're feeling super-fancy, you can also call it the "anagnorisis"! Whatever it's called, it's the moment where the main character realizes the true nature of their circumstances. As a result, that character has to decide how to solve their problem, whether to give up what they wanted at the beginning of the story or if they're willing to change something—to act—in order to get it. The result of that decision determines the outcome of the story. Generally, if the main character gets what they want, it's a happy ending. If not, well...

There's good news here: in the messaging you're putting together, there's never a tragic ending. You're designing a message that shows people that you have the answer to their question.

You're showing them how to get what they want, and often, how to get so much more.

With your work on the goal statement, you've determined something your audience wants. With your problem statement, you've defined the real problem that's getting in the way. I wish I could tell you that simply defining the problem is enough to create the change you're looking for... but I can't. There are likely endless examples of when you've known the "right" thing to do, but haven't done it or have put it off.

Why? It's a lesson I learned in the thirteen years I spent moonlighting as a Weight Watchers leader: you can't create change, only the conditions for it.

Sure, you can inspire someone to act. Depending on the situation, you could even force them. Action is occasional and, often, externally driven. But *change* is something quite different. It includes action, yes. But change is sustained action. It's also usually driven internally—by a person themselves. All you can do is set up the parameters that are likely to make that change happen.

How? Through conflict. Internal conflict. And specifically, a conflict between what someone wants (their goal) and what they believe to be true, about either themselves or the world around them. That conflict almost always puts people at odds with what they've been doing so far. That's what happened when people first heard "a diamond is forever" back in 1947. People couldn't ignore that a ring with a *forever-lasting* diamond was surely a better symbol than a ring without one. If they believed their commitment was forever, well then, they weren't going to go for amethyst. (Sorry, amethyst.)

That kind of conflict has a name: "cognitive dissonance." It's a technical name for what happens when two (or more) things we know to be true fight with each other. But, as I like to remind people, when two truths fight, only one lives. Our brains cannot really let conflicts like that stand. We will change in order to relieve that mental discomfort.

Conflict drives choice.

Choice drives change.

That's what your truth statement is meant to do: engineer a moment of truth that creates an internal conflict in your audience. It's going to use what your audience wants and what they believe (two things that don't change quickly) to put pressure on the one thing that *can* change in an instant: their perspective. When you create the conditions for the audience to change their perspective, you create the conditions for them to change their behavior, as well.

How to Build Your Truth Statement

Start with "why?"

The moment of truth is the midpoint of a story for a reason: it's the pivot point between the problem and the change. As such, it needs to explain why your problem is a problem—and especially, why the new perspective needs attention. Asking "why" is a good place to start.

→ **DO THIS**: Ask yourself, "Why is the problem such a problem?" or even, "Why is the new perspective so important?" (As ever, keep your brainstorms. You'll use them later!)

Draft a statement that meets the criteria listed at the beginning of the chapter.

If on the first try you arrive at a truth statement that meets the criteria I listed earlier, congratulations! I'm pretty sure you're a unicorn. The truth statement is almost always the hardest piece of your Red Thread to figure out. That's because it's often a belief, value, or assumption that is so core to who you are—it just seems so *obvious* to you—that it never occurs to you to articulate it.

That said, one of the best indicators that you've found the right problem pair is that you can immediately explain it with a truth statement, often without

CHOICE

DRIVES

CHANGE.

realizing it! For example, I was working with consultant and speaker Tracy Timm, and we had just identified her problem pair of "managers focusing on *positions* more than *people*." As soon as she said that, she added, "And that's crazy, because *people are what make the positions work*!" Voila! Truth statement.

Your first couple of answers will likely not meet the criteria above. Most often, I see people try to jump to the solution or start listing the benefits of a change. What you need to do here is keep pushing until you land on something that people can't argue with (at least not easily). How do you do that? Here are some techniques that work well with my clients and will likely work for you, too.

The Five Whys

You may have heard of the Five Whys exercise before. It originated with Sakichi Toyoda and the Toyota car company as part of their efforts to improve and streamline their manufacturing processes. As a key player in that evolution noted, when you ask "why" five times, "the nature of the problem, as well as its solution, becomes clear."[11] This exercise is one of those classic "simple but not easy" ones. You are basically going to ask yourself, "Why is the problem such a problem?" again, only this time you're going to ask the question "why" about your answer, five times over.

→ **DO THIS**: Ask yourself again: "Why is the problem such a problem?"

Take your answer (for example, "It's such a problem because it creates *y* effect"), and ask yourself "why" again: "Why does *x* create *y* effect?"

Repeat that pattern, using your previous answer in your next "why" question, five times or until you arrive at a "root" cause, a truth statement that meets the criteria.

My clients UrSure wanted to develop a Red Thread for an initial sales conversation (the application) with an audience of health care providers. For an outcome, they wanted those providers to agree to a trial of their product, a urine-testing kit. To do that, we needed a truth that would speak directly to the belief of patients and doctors that patients were taking a particular, non-detectable medication correctly, despite the probability that they were not. This truth would need to speak to the heart of the health care providers' problem: "having to rely more on what patients *recall* than what tests *reveal*." And we already knew what the recommended solution was: UrSure's urine tests.

But remember that the truth needs to explain why the problem is such a problem *and* why a solution is the right one. So, following the Five Whys exercise, we asked: "Why were urine tests the better answer?" Because there was no delay in getting the results. *Why was that better?* Because it closed the gap between what patients recalled and what tests revealed. *Why was that better?* Because the tests showed both patients and doctors whether the medication was present—they could turn effects people couldn't feel into results they could see. *Why was that better?* Because, to quote the old saying, "seeing is believing." And there it was. A truth that made the problem impossible to ignore.

Note that the "five" of the Five Whys is a bit arbitrary. The folks at Toyota found this was how many whys it took on average. You could find your root cause in fewer steps (especially if you're working with someone else who's fairly expert in this), or in more. Regardless, the point is to keep going until you get something that (1) your audience would readily agree with and (2) strongly ties your problem and your idea together.

Message math

Another technique that works well for arriving at your truth statement is reverse engineering the pieces of the Red Thread you've built so far. You have your idea. You also have your goal and problem pair. Along with the truth, those elements have this "mathematical" relationship:

▌ Goal + Problem + Truth = Idea (your Change)

Just as in stories, your idea (which we'll use synonymously with the change we'll discuss in the next chapter) is the logical conclusion of what's happened so far. It's the sum of the concepts you've introduced. If you're struggling to find your truth statement, treat it like a missing variable, and solve for it:

▌ Goal + Problem + x = Idea (your Change)

In other words, given the change you're building to, and what you've introduced so far with the goal and problem, what concept *must* the truth introduce? Once you've figured out what your truth needs to do, it's much easier to find what you need to say.

→ **DO THIS**: Solve for the truth as you would for a missing variable in a math equation. Ask yourself, "What concept *must* the truth add to the goal and problem so that the audience will see this idea as a logical conclusion?"

It's science!

The truth is something that your audience would agree with, about the world or themselves. What else fits that category? With most audiences, it's science. If someone agrees with a generally accepted principle of science (what goes up must come down; a body in motion stays in motion, a body at rest stays at rest; for every action, there's an equal and opposite reaction...) they're likely to agree with it as a metaphor in the context of your Red Thread. It's one of the reasons I think the De Beers slogan "a diamond is forever" has been so effective for so long. In most circumstances, that statement is literally true. When De Beers used it metaphorically, people "mapped over" that scientific belief to an emotional one.

You can use a scientific principle as is or adjust it with your own language (for example, "A *mind* in motion stays in motion; a mind at rest stays at rest"). Make sure, though, that your audience would still be likely to agree with your new version!

→ **DO THIS**: Brainstorm generally accepted principles of science and the natural world that speak to the same core concept as your truth.

Use one of these principles as is or modify it to craft your truth statement.

Axioms, idioms, quotes, and proverbs

While scientific principles have generally been proved through rigorous testing, other principles have been "proved" through people's own experiences. Every culture has widely accepted social truths that everyone tends to agree with. These social truths, captured most often in sayings that people repeat, are a rich source of potential truth statements. Why? Because people are inclined to agree with such go-to phrases and consider them the way life or the world is. They describe the "true nature" of people, the world, or a specific set of circumstances. As a result, you usually won't experience much, if any, resistance to them.

Where do you find those sayings? I often recommend that my clients start with their own or their companies' mantras. Those phrases that people say often to themselves or to each other almost always come from their baseline assumptions of how they see the world . . . from their *personal* truth statements. For instance, a number of proverbs guide my thinking:

- A stitch in time saves nine.
- What's good for the goose is good for the gander.
- The runner and the road are one with the errand to be done.

I've also developed some of my own over the years:

* Pain is the enemy of long-term change.
* How you see drives what you do.
* The biggest leaps start from the surest ground.

As with scientific principles, you can use these kinds of sayings as is or adjust them with your own language.

→ **DO THIS**: Brainstorm quotes, proverbs, and other generally accepted social truths that speak to the same core concept as your truth.

Use one of these sayings as is or modify it to create your truth statement.

The conclusions of published research

It's possible that you have done the research to prove something entirely new. Perhaps you've developed a unique proprietary approach that allows something that previously wasn't possible to be possible now. Or perhaps your research establishes something as true that people didn't previously know to be true.

In one such example, a TEDxCambridge speaker I worked with, Dheeraj Roy, had this truth statement: "It is possible to strengthen the memory retrieval system in mice with early-stage Alzheimer's." That's a new understanding of the world and how it works. Imagine you're a researcher looking for cures and treatments for Alzheimer's disease. If previously you'd focused only on whether or not memories still exist in people with Alzheimer's, and not how the memories are retrieved, this new insight would be pretty hard to ignore.

A quick note: Most professional and academic researchers are fundamentally uncomfortable with the idea that the truth statement is itself a "truth." Science in general resists the notion of universal truths like that. If you feel the same way, it may help to remember that the truth statement is called that because it creates a *moment* of truth. I shorten it to "truth" for efficiency (remember my "stitch in time" proverb?). I also recommend to my scientific and academic clients that they think of the truth more as an insight that people are likely to agree with.

Most conclusions of peer-reviewed, published research are viable truth statements, even if they are comparatively rare. Most people simply haven't done that kind of research unless they're an academic, scientist, or researcher to begin with or are an established organization with the size and funding for a research and development team. The "published" and "peer-reviewed" components are important, though, because the truth needs to be something that people can validate without you. Publication usually means someone else has vetted your research and agrees that it's valid.

⇒ **DO THIS**: If you or your organization have done relevant research on the topic, look for possible truth statements in the conclusions of your published research.

Beware an Early Change

The most common mistake in finding a truth statement is also the most understandable one. What is it? People try to squeeze their solution, the change, in as the truth:

> Despite the barriers we all know exist, the real problem is... *we focus on x, more than on y* [TWO-PART PROBLEM]. Yet we can all agree it's true that... *focusing on y is the answer* [WRONG TRUTH].

Nope. *Don't do this!* Don't make your idea your truth!

People need a "because." When you present your audience with a problem, yes, they need a solution. Before they'll accept that solution, though, they need to agree that the problem is *enough* of a problem to act on. You can't skip this step.

Lots of folks use a similar analogy, and it's useful to help me explain: Let's say you need a physical and you come to see me as your new doctor. Now imagine that, on your very first visit, and before I've even examined you, I ask you, "So, are you ready to schedule the surgery?" Of course, your answer would be, "Um, no..." because I've presented you with only a solution. Before you'll agree with and act on it, you need to know *why* you need the surgery. But even if I present you with a problem—"Hey, you have a spot on your back. Are you ready to schedule surgery?"—that's still not enough.

You need to hear something *about* the problem that makes it obvious why you need surgery. If I were actually a medical expert, I might be able to determine by sight that your spot is the kind you operate on. But if you as my patient don't have that expertise, either, or can't even see the spot, you wouldn't know or believe it. You'd have to hear something like, "That spot looks like the kind we need to operate on. Therefore, are you willing to let me do tests to see if that's necessary?"

At that point, you'd at least know why I thought the problem is such a problem. And notice, you probably still wouldn't be willing to jump to surgery. But you might be willing to do something (tests) that would lead in that direction.

Resolve the Conflict

Once you've found the truth of your Red Thread, you have all the pieces that connect your audience's question with your answer. The moment of truth forces your audience to choose:

* Give up what I want (my goal)?

* Give up how I've been looking for the answer (the problem)?

* Give up what I believe to be true about myself or the world (the truth)?

Those questions reflect the internal conflict your audience wants—and needs—to resolve. This is a critical point in their path to your idea. You want to keep your audience moving forward through the discomfort.

You don't want them to avoid it and fall back on their previous thinking and behavior.

That's why your next step is to present them with a restabilizing force. You need to present the choice that will help them achieve their goal, the choice that concludes your case. Your next step is to present the change they need to make. Whether or not they realize it, you've presented them with clues about what to do next, but now you need to make the answer—your idea—clear.

Steps Through the Maze (aka Action Items!)

To find the truth statement of your Red Thread, have you:

☐ Found the single, core concept that explains both the problem and the answer your idea represents?

☐ Turned that core concept into a proverb-like statement?

☐ If you're struggling, tried the Five Whys, "message math," and looked to pre-existing proverbs, the world of science, or your own published research?

(6)

THE
CHANGE

⸻

GOAL: Build the story of change people will tell themselves (so you can turn your idea into action, and maybe even change the world).

PROBLEM: To make the story truly their own, your audience needs more than an answer to their question about their goal. They need the agency to choose that answer themselves.

TRUTH: Counterintuitive as it may be, less choice leads to more action.

CHANGE: Offer your audience a simple, single change that's consistent with what they want and believe.

ACTION: Draft the change statement of your Red Thread.

GRASP ALL,
LOSE ALL

What Is the Change Statement?

At its simplest, the *change statement* is your idea, your answer to your audience's question (their goal). It is the high-level shift in thinking or behavior that you're asking your audience to take. Your change statement should fit comfortably in this sentence:

> That's why, to achieve the goal, we need to... [CHANGE].

Here are some stellar examples of change statements: "That's why, to achieve the goal, we need to...

* make the invisible, visible, instantly—we need to turn the effects people can't feel into results they can see."

* pair Big Data with 'Thick' Data—data and insights drawn from what Big Data doesn't (and can't) track."

* adopt this project as a way to both increase who sees our content, and through the revenue it generates, increase our capacity for content output."

* address the imprints from our past experiences that are still lodged as fear in our bodies."

- personalize incentives to the people in positions."

- do scary stuff *on purpose*, every day."

- develop Multi-Level Leadership—leadership at every level."

The De Beers "a diamond is forever" tagline created a change in the story people told themselves about engagement rings: to see the stone as the symbol, not just the ring. That change resolves the conflict that the truth, "a diamond is forever," introduced:

> We can all agree we want to know the best symbol of our commitment we can give to each other. Despite the barriers we all know exist, the real problem is a ring is a symbol, but the kind of ring can be a symbol, too. Yet we can agree it's true that a diamond is forever. That's why, to achieve the goal, we need to see the stone as the symbol, not just the ring.

That change of "seeing the stone as the symbol" allowed engaged couples to still (1) have the "best" symbol of their commitment, (2) use a ring to represent it, and (3) still believe both the literal and metaphorical interpretations of "a diamond is forever." In fact, that combination of concepts allowed couples to grab onto what felt like an even better version of the story they were already telling themselves: "Our commitment is now *extra* forever, because it's both a ring and a diamond!"

Notice that De Beers never had to overtly say, "See the stone as the symbol." The tagline "a diamond is forever" was enough: the audience's story-seeking brains filled in the rest. When it comes to getting people to act on your big idea, though, you don't want to leave the change to chance.

KISS (Keep It Simple, Smartie!)

Change is a funny thing. As you now already know, you can't create change, only the conditions for it. That's what you've done with your truth statement—you've created a conflict that your audience needs to resolve. So prompting the change you want is the next, easy step, right? All you have to do is tell your audience what change they need to make, and they will . . . won't they?

CHANGE STATEMENT CRITERIA

1. The change statement is more than a simple reverse of the problem; it's the conclusion of all you've introduced so far.

2. As such, it flows in logic, concepts, and language from the other three statements.

3. It resolves the tension between the two parts of your problem pair.

4. It contains only one shift in thinking or behavior.

5. The actions you'll introduce next logically fit within it.

6. It's a realistic shift, given where your audience started.

Well, maybe. Particularly if you give them the option not to change.

Huh?

Yes, you read that right. When you give your audience a choice to *not* do what you want them to do, they're more likely to change the way you want them to. Counterintuitive as it may be, it's how the human brain works.

One of the most important conditions for change is that a person feels in control of themselves, their lives, or their choices.

This is a concept psychologists call "agency." When it comes to action or changing, agency is everything. If people don't feel like they have a choice, that they're being told what to do, their natural reaction is to push back. You probably had this feeling as a child when a parent or guardian told you to do something. Even if it was something that you wanted to do, the fact that you were *told* to do it made you want to refuse. *News flash:* We never grow out of that instinct.

That tendency to say no when told what to do is what you've worked so hard to avoid triggering with your Red Thread. It's why you started with something your audience already wanted. It's why you framed the problem in a way that validates their current views. It's why you chose a truth they could confirm without you. So, now that you've reached the conclusion of all that work—your change—you've got to avoid that "no" now. And to do that, you have to give people a choice.

But not too many choices! That's because of another funny trick of the brain: the more choices you give someone, the less likely that they'll choose at all.[12] Why? With an excess of "nos" floating around in their heads, people are much more likely to stick with what makes them feel smart, capable, and good. More often than not, that means they'll stick with what they were already doing, even if it isn't working.

This presents a puzzle, I know. You can't give someone no choice or you remove their agency and trigger a refusal of your idea. If you give them too many choices, they'll take their agency and choose the status quo.

What can you do? Give your audience the option of a simple, *single* change that's consistent with what they want and believe. When UrSure presents their change, "turn the effects people can't feel into results they can see," it arrives as a single, logical conclusion of their case. If doctors want their patients to stay on the medications they don't feel the effects of, agree that delayed tests aren't ideal, and believe that "seeing is believing," the option of making results visible—and instant—seems "right," both logically and emotionally. UrSure's approach follows logic and it validates doctors' own lived experience of the world.

Since your Red Thread is the case for your idea, the change you'll recommend is your idea itself. The change is your answer to your audience's question (their goal). Since you've built your case on what your audience already agrees is true, it's much more likely that they'll agree with your change, as well.

But keep it simple! Your audience has one big question, which means they're looking for one big

ONE OF THE MOST IMPORTANT

CONDITIONS FOR CHANGE

IS THAT A PERSON FEELS IN

CONTROL OF THEMSELVES, THEIR

LIVES, OR THEIR CHOICES.

———————————

answer—not five. While you may offer multiple products that deliver on your change, or there may be multiple steps in your model, people need to agree with the underlying meaning of your idea, first. By providing that, you're giving them the answer they're looking for *and* the agency to disagree with it.

Yes, your audience may disagree with your change. But you've given them the choice, and you must, to respect and uphold their agency. Given that their other choices include ignoring the evidence in front of them, unwanting something they want, or unbelieving something they believe, it's more likely than not they'll choose the change you present.

How to Build Your Change Statement

In many ways, your change statement should be the easiest one to build. After all, it *is* your idea—or at least one aspect of it. That said, my clients sometimes struggle with this step because they want so badly to introduce *all* the things people need to do to achieve their goal. At heart, however, the steps for building a change statement are simple (even if not always easy).

⇢ **DO THIS**: Identify the simple, single shift in thinking or behavior that will help your audience achieve their goal. (*Hint:* You may have already done this with your answer to "What is your idea?" so go back to your notes from the first chapter and review your answer to that question.)

If that idea works as part of your Red Thread (and it likely does), ask yourself, "How do I need to adapt it to make it fit with the goal, problem, and truth I've introduced?"

Turn your answer into a statement that satisfies the criteria for a change statement.

Resolve the tension

A good way to find your change is to resolve the tension between the two parts of your problem pair. For example, my client Tracy Timm's Red Thread (featured in the examples throughout this book) had the problem pair "managers focusing on *positions* more than *people*." Because her truth was that "it's the people that make positions work," she resolved the tension with this change: "*personalize incentives to the people in positions*—offer options associated with different functions or job levels."

Instead of saying "stop focusing on positions and focus on people instead" (which is just a reverse of the problem, a no-no in your Red Thread!), she found a way to make both perspectives on the problem work together. The problem is now solved, there's a clear way for her audience to achieve their goal, and all of it works with the truth her audience already believes ("people are what make positions work").

→ **DO THIS**: Revisit your two-part problem statement and ask yourself, "What change can people make that combines the two perspectives?"

Turn your answer into a statement that satisfies the criteria for a change statement.

Roll up your actions

If neither approach above produces immediate results, flip to the next chapter, on actions. Sometimes discovering your change is easier once you know the actions you want your audience to take. Why does that work? Well, it's back to the "message math" I talked about in the previous chapter:

▌ **Goal + Problem + Truth = Idea (your Change)**

But now we can add one more piece of information:

▌ **Goal + Problem + Truth = Idea (your Change) = Actions**

Just as the change equals the sum of your goal, problem, and truth, your change also equals actions. In other words, if people put your actions in place, they will have changed. For example, my client Andrea Fryrear, the CEO of her company AgileSherpas, already had a proven model—the Marketing Agility Ascension—for helping businesses apply the Agile practices originally created for rapid software development to their marketing approach. The model has four clear stages—actions—starting with tasks like identifying metrics and planning a pilot project, all the way through to training internal champions and comparing pre- and post-performance measures.

Even though Andrea knew already what her model is (the four stages) and what it does for her clients (helps them apply Agile practices to marketing), she didn't yet know how to describe the "big idea" behind it—the change it represents, both for her clients and the market. To find that change, we performed a little message math.

Andrea's audience is marketing leaders who want to take their organizations Agile. Here are the Red Thread statements we developed:

> We all want to know how to apply Agile practices to our marketing work (GOAL). While there are barriers we all know exist, the real problem is focusing on Agile projects instead of Agile teams (TWO-PART PROBLEM). Yet we can agree it's true people persist long after projects end (TRUTH).

Using the elements from both the statements so far and her Marketing Agility Ascension model, we realized the change needed to include

* something about practices,

* something that resolved the tension between projects and teams, and

* something that spoke to persistence *over time*.

That led us to this change statement: "Instead of part-time pilots of Agile practices, build persistent teams of Agile practitioners...," which is what her model is designed to do.

If you're like Andrea and have already figured out what your actions are, step back mentally and ask yourself what that change is.

→ **DO THIS**: Flip to the next chapter and determine your actions.

With your actions collected, ask yourself, "If people performed these actions, what change will they have made? What shift in thinking or behavior do these actions represent?"

Turn your answer into a statement that satisfies the criteria for a change statement.

Making the Concepts Concrete

Even if you weren't sure how to effectively express your idea when you started this book, by the time you reach the change, you do—or you're getting pretty close to it. You've made the answer to your audience's goal question clear. With the truth, you've also made inaction on the two-part problem almost impossible. Instead of a dizzying array of choices, you've presented a simple, single new choice—one that's far more attractive to them than giving up their goal, ignoring evidence, or bailing on a long-standing belief.

Your audience should now *want* to make the change you offer. They want to put it into action. But to do that, they need the change to be concrete. Luckily, that's exactly what you'll do in the next chapter.

Steps Through the Maze (aka Action Items!)

To find the change statement of your Red Thread, have you:

☐ Summarized the simple, single shift in thinking or behavior that will help your audience achieve their goal?

☐ Revisited your original answer to "What is your idea?"

☐ If you're struggling, used "message math" to arrive at your change statement by applying your actions? (You'll need to jump ahead to the next chapter to do this, and that's fine, as long as you don't forget to finish this step afterward.)

(7)

THE
ACTION(S)

GOAL: Build the story of change people will tell themselves (so you can turn your idea into action, and maybe even change the world).

PROBLEM: For a story to drive action, it needs to explain not only why a change is necessary, but also how to make that change.

TRUTH: Details make the conceptual concrete.

CHANGE: Use details to give your audience enough information to act on your idea.

ACTION: Draft your action set.

IMAGINARY MILLS GRIND NO FLOUR

––––––––––

What Are the Actions?

Actions answer the question "How...?" This can include questions like, "How do I make the change?" "How do you help *me* make the change?" and "How do I know I've been successful?" Because the actions make the change concrete for your audience, they are necessary for the change to happen. The good news? If you've already developed your idea into an approach or a suite of products or services, you already have your actions. (Or at least one set of them!)

The actions follow your change statement (That's why, to achieve the goal, we need to... [CHANGE]) and should fit comfortably in this sentence:

▌ Here's how: [ACTIONS].

Some examples of action statements and action sets (multiple actions) are: "Here's how:

* Create simple urine tests that providers administer during their patient's visits."

* Use people like ethnographers and researchers to collect and interpret data that can't be quantified, like stories, emotions, and interactions."

* Create a new editorial position of newsletter editor."

* There are four steps: (1) Identify and deactivate past experiences. (2) Change the language we use in the stories we tell ourselves about what's happening. (3) Reconnect with the enjoyment of being the center of attention. (4) Build capacity to tolerate new, more positive feelings."

* Offer *options* associated with different functions or job levels. For example, someone at a more junior level could choose between one day of remote work every month or one additional day of personal time off. Someone at a higher level could choose between three days."

* Conduct Fear Experiments, which have these components: focus, energy, action, repeat."

* Help your team progress through each of four levels: contributor, coach, developer, pioneer."

With De Beers and diamond rings, the action step of the hypothetical Red Thread we've been building is simple: "Buy a diamond engagement ring." When we add that to the end of what we've built so far, we get:

> We can all agree we want to know the best symbol of
> our commitment we can give to each other. Despite
> the barriers we all know exist, the real problem is a
> ring is a symbol, but the kind of ring can be a sym-
> bol, too. Yet we can agree it's true that a diamond is
> forever. That's why, to achieve the goal, we need to

> see the stone as the symbol, not just the ring. Here's
> how: buy a diamond engagement ring.

As time wore on, and as the tagline took root, De Beers applied "forever" in all sorts of extensions. For instance, diamonds are now a way to celebrate children's births, anniversaries, and even a solo commitment to yourself. Before De Beers even coined "a diamond is forever," they developed actions, with the "4 Cs"—color, cut, clarity, and carat weight—which, yep, De Beers helped invent and popularize.[13] De Beers also spread the common wisdom about how much someone should spend on a ring (another action): back in the 1930s it was one month's salary, in the 1980s it was two, and these days it's three.[14] (Are you annoyed about this story yet?!)

ACTIONS CRITERIA

1. Actions contain at least one specific element that makes the change concrete.

2. They can be classified as processes, components, criteria, or categories (more on these types, below).

3. They tie back to the concepts and language of your goal, problem, and truth.

From Understanding to Action

Turning your ideas into action is the whole point of building your Red Thread. In fact, defining the actions you want your audience to take so you can achieve your outcome is how you make your Red Thread measurable. If your audience responds to your call to action, you were successful; if they don't... well, then you have some more work to do.

Much of the content I see, though, stops at "understanding" an idea as its objective. The content creator presents enough information to describe the idea, but not necessarily enough to move the audience to action. Yet there's a huge difference between learning what something is *conceptually* and experiencing it in reality. Think, for instance, about learning from the Merriam-Webster dictionary that a peach is a "single-seeded drupe with a hard central stone, a pulpy white or yellow flesh, and a thin fuzzy skin" and tasting one for the first time.

But how do you create experience when someone is only reading or hearing about your idea? Or when the change you're asking them for needs to happen long after you've written the page they're reading or you've left the room?

By describing the change as closely to the experience of it as possible.

Let's go back to the peach. If someone has never had one before, the more information you give them about the experience of eating a peach, the more likely they may be to try one. But not just information like "single-seeded drupe," right? It needs to be concrete. Even better if you can associate it with something they've had before: "It's kind of like an orange, but with the soft, smooth flesh of a cherry." "It's juicy like a pineapple." If that sounds good to them, they'd probably also appreciate practical information like, "You can eat the skin." "There's a pit in the center, which you can just eat around." "Eat it over the sink, because it's literally *that* juicy." The more details you give, the more concrete the imagined experience will be.

To create that experience, there are three things in particular that your audience needs to understand and agree with before they'll act on your change. What are they? First, that it's *possible* to achieve the goal with the change you recommend. So, you need to give your audience examples. They need to read, see, or hear stories and testimonials of your product, your service, or your idea helping others achieve the goal your audience also wants.

Second, your audience needs to believe that it's possible *for them*. You need to map the experiences of others onto your audience and their specific situation. This is where hands-on demonstrations of your idea come in handy, even something as simple as asking them to imagine where in their life the idea could work.

Third, your audience needs to believe that the actions are *worth it*. Whenever you're asking someone to change their thinking or behavior, you're literally asking them to rewire their brains (to tell themselves a new and different story). If you're talking to a prospective customer, you're also asking them to part with some of their money. So, they need to feel that the benefit of the change outweighs the risks or costs of it. Those risks and costs can be in effort, money, time, or even reputation. Your audience needs enough detail to determine that risk–reward equation for themselves.

Details make the change more concrete and actionable. Those details are the actions of your Red Thread.

How to Build Your Actions

Step 1: Brainstorm your action types

Actions fall into four basic types: processes, components, criteria, and categories. Which you choose will depend on your application, audience, and outcome.

For example, let's say your idea has something to do with artificial intelligence (AI). The actions for a keynote or TEDx talk could be the steps you want your audience to take to start engaging with AI (identify routine tasks you currently do manually, research AI products and services that perform those tasks, choose one to pilot, and so on). In a pitch to investors, remember that those investors need the actions to agree that the change is possible. They need to believe that your company is *capable* of creating the change you've presented to them—that it's possible. In that case, the actions may be steps you or your company take or products and services you offer to help a different audience than the investors to achieve their goal (a quiz to help potential clients identify routine tasks, a "device match" service to help turn someone's quiz results into products to research, a "try at home" program to determine fit, and so on). If that part of your pitch is successful, you could follow with the next steps for the investors to take with you or describe how you're planning on using the investments you receive.

Even if one particular type of action below seems clearly to be the right fit for your application, begin by brainstorming options for all the categories. The extra material adds depth, breadth, and length to your exploration and you can use it later, in different applications. If, for instance, you use this process to develop a thirty-minute keynote—and you've done the work of brainstorming all these extra pieces—you don't miss a step if someone asks you to speak for an additional sixty minutes. Or if your pitch to investors was successful, you can lay out the steps your audience can take to move the project forward.

With some of my clients, brainstorming the actions has led to a much deeper understanding of the scope of their idea, to identifying new models they could trademark, and to ideas for new products and services, as well.

So, let's explore each action type.

Process actions are exactly what you'd think: the sequential steps needed to create the change. In my experience, they are the most common form of actions. Process actions are almost always stated as verbs and usually in stepwise order. An example from my childhood: stop, drop, and roll, which was how I was taught to respond if I ever found myself on fire. The Red Thread method can itself be a process: Find the goal, problem, truth, change, and actions... in that order.

→ **DO THIS**: To find process actions, ask yourself, "What steps are necessary to create the change?"

The next most common type is *component actions*. These are similar to steps in that they describe what's needed to make the change happen, but the component elements can happen in any order. Component actions are almost always stated as nouns. For example, when I was a Weight Watchers leader, the program had three major components: food, activity, and mindset. All three are necessary to "live a healthier lifestyle" (the change), but they don't have to happen in sequence. You don't work on activity, then food, then mindset. You work on all three at once, or on whichever will help you most. Components can also describe your offerings, products, or services, as in, "Here's how we [your company] create that change: through consulting, publishing, and training."

→ **DO THIS**: To find component actions, ask yourself, "What elements need to be in place? What is required to make this real, no matter the order?"

Slightly less common are *criteria actions*. These describe the qualities of a successful change, much like you'd describe a summer day as "warm, sunny, and relaxed." Criteria actions are usually stated as adjectives. For example, I often describe successful

DETAILS
MAKE THE
CONCEPTUAL
CONCRETE.

messages as having four criteria: they are relevant, resilient, remarkable, and repeatable.

→ **DO THIS**: To find criteria actions, ask yourself, "What qualities or traits describe a successful change?"

The final type is *category actions*. These are the areas (departments, levels, phases...) where the change can or should be applied. You can use category actions to describe what your change looks like in different areas of an organization (the sales department versus the marketing department) or in life (as in personally, professionally, globally—to borrow from my friend, speaker and author Neen James).[15]

→ **DO THIS**: To find category actions, ask yourself, "What are all the applications of the change? What are all the areas in which it can be applied?"

Step 2: Pick your type

Once you've brainstormed all your action options, one type usually rises to the top as fitting best for the application you chose. All you have to do in this step is pick one!

→ **DO THIS**: Based on the application you chose, decide which action type you'll use. (As before, keep your brainstorms. You'll want them for future applications.)

If there isn't a clear winner for your type yet, don't worry, just go to the next step. Sometimes additional refinement clarifies the choice.

Step 3: Narrow the choices

While I recommend you always include at least one concrete action in your Red Thread, there's an upper limit, too. Remember from the last chapter that the greater the choice, the lower the chance of change? Yep, that still applies. That's why I suggest you narrow down your actions to no more than five of any one type, with three being the magic number. People have trouble remembering any more than that, so focus their attention on the most critical information only.

Can you break this rule and give your audience seven elements or twelve steps? Of course, but make sure your application supports it. The more elements or steps, the more content you'll need to explain them—and that might well suit a workshop or a book. If time or space is limited, keep your list of actions short.

→ **DO THIS**: Narrow down your brainstormed actions to one to five options per type.

Step 4: Modify for memorability

Once you know the concepts of your actions, start working on how to make them work well in people's ears with the same techniques you used with your problem pair:

* Alliteration ("assess, articulate, activate")
* Assonance ("try, find, fight")
* Rhyme ("know, go, flow")
* Patterns of syllables ("inspiration, activation")

As with your problem pair, working with prosody can help you find your actions, and the rhythm and sounds of your action titles can help your audience remember them better, too.

→ **DO THIS**: With your narrowed list of actions, play with a group of descriptive words that work together as an alliterative, rhythmical, or similar type of "poetic" (and thus memorable) set.

Step 5: Name it to claim it

Sometimes it makes sense to name your set of actions or the model that represents them. That's what I did when I called the model you're working with now the Red Thread. It's also what my client Ted Ma did with his model of four levels of leadership when he called it Multi-Level Leadership.

Such names can come from all sorts of places. The "red thread" already existed as an idiom to describe what *my* Red Thread builds. Multi-Level Leadership drew from my client's differentiating background in multi-level marketing. You can also pull potential names from the language you've introduced in your pre-existing branding or from phrases or metaphors you use regularly.

→ **DO THIS**: Develop a name for your action set. Draw from the language you've used so far in your Red Thread, relevant metaphors, idioms, other expressions, and your branding.

A branded or trademarkable name for your action set is definitely not required, but it can help establish thought leadership and differentiate your work.

Mix, Match, Maximize

As you brainstorm your action types, you may start to notice something: more than one type can apply to your change. In fact, you'll often want, or even need, to "mix and match" your action types. For example, for the Red Thread, I've presented to you a five-step process: find the goal, then the problem, then the truth, then the change, then your actions. And I've told you the criteria for making your change successful: a great message is relevant, resilient, remarkable, and repeatable. In chapter 9, The Red Thread Storyline, I'll explain how to adapt the framing and tense of your Red Thread statements for two different categories: whether you're explaining an idea or selling it.

If you're constructing a message to be strong enough to build a book, workshop, or business on, you may need to have the broad, solid foundation these kinds of combinations provide. The options are nearly endless. But they're often not necessary. If your message is brief and your change simple, don't overcomplicate it!

•

The Practical End of Your Red Thread

Regardless of how you arrive at them, your actions represent the practical end of your Red Thread. You've moved your audience from their initial question through an understanding of the real problem, brought them a truth that forced a choice, presented a change that achieved their goal, and given them the actions to take to make that change real.

Next up? Showing how that mental journey may have brought them more than they realized.

Steps Through the Maze (aka Action Items!)

To find the actions of your Red Thread, have you:

☐ Brainstormed options for each of the four action types?

☐ Determined which action type works best for your application?

☐ Narrowed your action set to one to five options?

☐ Experimented with prosody for your actions and considered naming your actions or turning them into a model?

(8)

THE GOAL
REVISITED

GOAL: Build the story of change people will tell themselves (so you can turn your idea into action, and maybe even change the world).

PROBLEM: Great stories create tension between what someone wants and what they need. Happy endings resolve that tension.

TRUTH: Humans love happy endings because they fulfill expectations of the way things "should" be—namely, that being smart, capable, and good deserves a reward.

CHANGE: Show your audience the happy ending ahead of them, and what else they've gained in the process.

ACTION: Build your goal revisited.

A POINT IS THE

BEGINNING

OF MAGNITUDE

What Is the Goal Revisited?

The *goal revisited* shows your audience what else they will gain by making the change. It reveals possibilities above and beyond your audience's original goal. It usually follows your change and/or actions (That's why, to achieve the goal, we need to ... [CHANGE]. Here's how: [ACTIONS]), and should fit comfortably in this sentence:

> Not only does that achieve the goal, it also ... [GOAL REVISITED].

Here are some examples: "Not only does that achieve the goal, it also ...

* empowers patients and providers to create personalized treatment plans and better outcomes."

* gives companies ownable insights that could potentially improve their business and transform their industries."

* creates a new potential revenue stream that would support both the editorial and financial missions of our organization."

* opens up a way for you to 'delight in the limelight' and be unapologetically *you*."

- drives the best and brightest performers—from any generation—to you as the new industry standard for a great place to work."

- means you can live a life of no regrets."

- helps you create a culture of leadership."

There are a number of ways to interpret the goal revisited of the story of diamond engagement rings. Usually when I tell the De Beers story, I use this combination (or some variant) of these Red Thread statements:

> We can all agree we want to know the best symbol of our commitment we can give to each other. Despite the barriers we all know exist, the real problem is a ring is a symbol, but the kind of ring can be a symbol, too. Yet we can agree it's true that a diamond is forever. That's why, to achieve the goal, we need to see the stone as the symbol, not just the ring. Here's how: buy a diamond engagement ring. Not only does that achieve the goal, it also leaves a legacy of your love that will last for generations.

For many, that's certainly one of the implied "free prizes" of a diamond: the idea that you can pass it down to your children. But a goal revisited for De Beers could be any one of those that the company uses in their advertising now, like "a diamond as unique as your love." That one makes me laugh because these days the popularity of diamonds suffers a bit from the very success of the 1947 campaign: a diamond may be forever, *but everyone has one.* (Diamonds are also now strongly associated with gender normative ideas of marriage, so the "story" of diamonds isn't necessarily as strong as it once was.) So, you can see how De Beers is trying to answer that, with piling on a new truth: that every diamond is unique … so your symbol can be forever and one-of-a-kind.

Ultimately, though, the success of De Beers comes down to the fact that they gave people what they wanted (a symbol) and so much more (a symbol that sends a message).

Finding the "Free Prize Inside"

Editor of bestselling books and storytelling expert Shawn Coyne explains that most great stories have at least two stories going on at once.[16] The primary story is driven by the main character's "conscious object of desire"—something tangible the main character knows they want. The main character's pursuit of that goal dictates the major plot points and drives the story forward … just like your audience's desire to achieve their goal drives their interest in your Red Thread.

But remember how your goal had to be a question your audience would ask out loud and to other people? And how in your heart of hearts you knew there was a deeper, more important question that they were really asking? That's what Coyne refers to as the "*sub*conscious object of desire." In fiction writing, that second, often intangible pursuit drives a second story that lives below the surface of the first one. One of the best

THE STORY OF
YOUR IDEA DOESN'T
REALLY END UNTIL
YOU TIE IT BACK
TO THE BEGINNING.

Christmas movies of all time (and I'll fight you on this), *Die Hard*, gives us a great example of both. The main story is, of course, about John McClane battling the bad guys occupying Nakatomi Plaza. The second story is about John and his relationship with his estranged wife, Holly, who happens to be one of the hostages of the aforementioned bad guys. The interplay between the two stories is what gives fiction—and frankly, all narratives—interest and depth.

As consumers of those stories we sense both going on, but it's usually not until the end that we realize the second one was there. Yet, more often than not, the ending of that second story is the one that hooks us. It's the one that makes us feel joy or despair. (I mean, *come on:* when John unclasps the watch from Holly's wrist so that best-villain-ever Hans Gruber falls to his death? You're cheering not just for the defeat of the bad guys, but for Holly, John, and the hope that all reconciliations represent. Yippee-ki-yay!)

Sometimes in stories someone gets what they want but not what they need—gets the celebrity they always wanted, but loses the love of their life—and the "win" feels like a hollow victory. If someone doesn't get what they want or need, then we're unsure of what will happen to this person we've come to care about and we often fear for the worst. And if someone does get that "subconscious object of desire"? Well, then we feel confident that the character will succeed because they now have what they *really* need, even if it isn't what they wanted in the first place.

GOAL REVISITED CRITERIA

1. The goal revisited must be something of clear value to your audience.

2. It should exceed the scale and scope of the original goal.

3. Often, it indicates a new potential goal for your audience.

If they get what they want *and* need, then we're delighted, just as we would be to discover (to borrow from the great marketing mind of Seth Godin) the "free prize inside" of our morning box of cereal.[17] It's like an added bonus. Humans *love* this kind of happy ending because it fulfills the expectations we have for the way things "should" be. If you're smart, capable, and good, our brains tell us, then you should get what you want and need. If you're not, you shouldn't. When your audience is the star of the story and they achieve their goal (and maybe gain something even better), you confirm for them that all-important human want and belief.

It's for all those reasons that the story of your idea doesn't really end until you tie it back to the beginning, to the goal your audience was looking for in the first place. In other words, even though the path to find the Red Thread is linear (Goal → Problem → Truth → Change → Action), when you tell the story of the Red Thread, it's circular (figure 3).

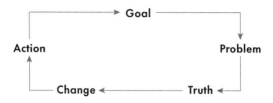

Figure 3: The circular path of the Red Thread

Coming back to the goal allows your audience to see they've succeeded in getting an answer to their original question—and, if there's one to be had, what the free prize inside is. That additional bonus of new benefits to enjoy, new questions to ask, or new paths to explore serves as the epilogue to the story of your idea. It shows your audience what happens after the story and what could now be in store for them.

How to Build Your Goal Revisited

The goal revisited serves as a way to show your audience what could be next for them if they make the change. It can reveal something several steps beyond where they are now or even beyond the scope of what they would have previously considered or dreamed of.

→ **DO THIS**: Ask yourself, "If the audience achieves this goal with this change, what else could they receive, achieve, or accomplish?"

Turn your best answer into a statement that satisfies the criteria for the goal revisited.

You might find that you've already built your goal revisited. Remember when you were working on defining your audience's goal? And I said that the audience's goal needs to be what your audience says they want, not what you think they want? That was probably a little bit frustrating, I know. But guess what? In the goal revisited, you can reveal what your audience *really* wants or needs.

Look back over your brainstorms when you were finding your audience's goal in chapter 3. The goal revisited may be lurking in the questions you thought the audience *should* be asking, even though they weren't asking them yet. Another place to look is to your notes (also from chapter 3) when you were thinking about the high-level "wants" behind their questions. (For example, "How can we improve patient outcomes?" "How can we improve profitability?" "How can we keep our community engaged and informed?") If the want didn't turn into the goal, it's likely a great candidate for the goal revisited.

⇒ **DO THIS**: Revisit your previous goal statement brainstorms, looking for a goal or question that meets the criteria for the goal revisited.

Turn your best answer into your goal revisited statement.

The "Call to Emotion"

You've no doubt heard the phrase "call to action." In this case, it's the specific ask you make of your audience so they can achieve their goal (and, ideally, help *you* achieve your outcome). That call usually derives from the action you outlined in the previous chapter.

As much as you may want your audience to be fully rational beings, carefully making the most logical decision based on the case you've made … they won't. Humans aren't rational decision-makers, they're rationalizing decision-makers. We decide based on gut, emotion, and instinct and then only later convince ourselves that what we chose to do (or not do) made rational sense.

The Red Thread is designed to work at both the intuitive (emotional) and intellectual (rational) levels. Part of someone's "gut check" on a new idea comes down to whether it tracks with the stories they have in their head. Are all the pieces there? Are they in the right order? And critically, does the story align with what I know about the stories I tell myself?

While those sound like rational, logical questions, they're all happening pre-consciously. If your brain produces a "no" to any of those questions in that pre-conscious phase, only the "no" makes it through to your conscious thought—not the reasoning behind the "no." That's why any case for your idea has to include all the pieces of that story structure your brain is trying to find. Your audience finds in your message what their brains are looking for and provides the "emotional" or "intuitive" response of "Yes, I feel good about this."

That doesn't let you or your message off the hook, though. The rationalizing phase still happens. That's why you've worked so hard as you've built your Red Thread to anchor all the pieces in both logic *and* belief. You tied your idea to something your audience wants. You found a pair of perspectives they could acknowledge and agree with. You anchored a change in a truth they could validate without you. You made your message resilient enough to withstand the rationalization that is the ultimate arbiter of whether or not someone acts.

You made your idea make sense.

But it never hurts to make your audience feel good about the choice, to close the circle back to the emotion that made them willing to say "yes" in the first place.

Your goal revisited does just that. It calls to that emotion and can be a powerful pair with a call to action: "If you do this, you'll achieve your goal (CALL TO ACTION)... and you just may also gain this goal revisited (CALL TO EMOTION)." Toward the end of the TEDx talk I worked on with Tricia Wang (one of the running examples in this book), she wraps up a story about how Netflix used an insight about viewers' binge-watching habits to revamp its entire approach to content delivery and user experience. She concludes with a line that presents the goal and goal revisited beautifully: "By integrating Big Data and 'Thick' Data (Tricia's CHANGE), they not only improved their business (GOAL), but they transformed how we consume

HUMANS AREN'T
RATIONAL DECISION-
MAKERS. THEY'RE
RATIONALIZING
DECISION-MAKERS.

media (GOAL REVISITED)." Tricia's implication for her audience is clear: Thick Data has the potential to transform industries.

Is the goal revisited required? Actually, no, it isn't. Your audience's brain knows the story is over as soon as you show how the change and actions help them achieve their goal (and they accept those actions as possible for them and worth it). But the call to emotion may be exactly what they need to feel that inaction is impossible.

Putting It All Together

Congratulations! You now have all the pieces of your idea's Red Thread.

* You've established a GOAL, something your audience wants.
* You've introduced a PROBLEM they didn't know they had.
* You've revealed a TRUTH that makes the problem impossible to ignore.
* You've defined the CHANGE needed to achieve the goal.
* And you've described the ACTION that creates the change.

With the goal revisited, you've taken that linear thread and tied it up with an emotional bow. You've not only shown your audience that they have what they need to succeed now, you've also painted the picture of what's possible next.

Now it's time to put all the pieces together. It's time to build the storyline of your idea.

Steps Through the Maze (aka Action Items!)

To find the goal revisited of your Red Thread, have you:

☐ Summarized what your audience would gain in addition to their goal as a result of making the change?

☐ If you're struggling, revisited your previous brainstorms of goal and audience want? (Great options often hide there!)

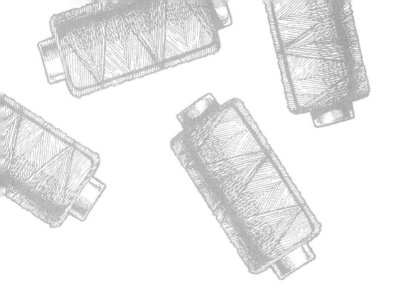

COMBI

PART

3

NATIONS

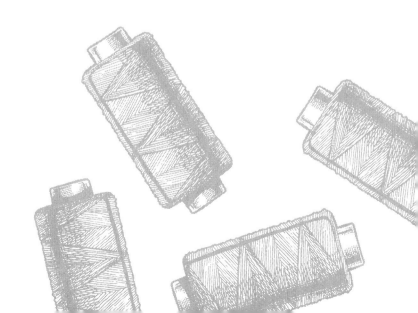

(9)

THE RED THREAD STORYLINE

GOAL: Build the story of change people will tell themselves (so you can turn your idea into action, and maybe even change the world).

PROBLEM: The function of a story matters as much as its form. Stories give people a way to explain cause and effect—*why* a certain action drives a certain result.

TRUTH: A story is an argument for an idea, for why your change achieves the audience's goal.

CHANGE: When you find the story of an idea, you also build the case for it.

ACTION: Draft the storyline of your idea.

NO STRENGTH
WITHIN,
NO STRENGTH
WITHOUT

What Is the Red Thread Storyline?

The *Red Thread Storyline* consists of all the pieces of your Red Thread, now strung together in (a very short) story form. As such, it's the "minimum viable case" for your idea. It combines all the previous statements into this paragraph:

> We can all agree we want to know... [GOAL]. Despite the barriers we all know exist, the real problem is... [TWO-PART PROBLEM]. Yet we can agree it's true that... [TRUTH]. That's why, to achieve the goal, we need to... [CHANGE]. Here's how: [ACTIONS]. Not only does that achieve the goal, it also... [GOAL REVISITED].

Here are the full Red Thread Storylines of the examples we've been looking at throughout:

* "We can all agree we want to know how we can keep patients on critical medications longer. Despite the barriers we all know exist, the real problem is having to rely more on what patients recall than what tests reveal. Yet we can agree it's true that 'seeing is believing.' That's why, to achieve the goal, we need to make the invisible, visible, instantly—we need to

turn the effects people can't feel into results they can see. Here's how: Create simple urine tests that providers administer during their patient's visits. Not only does that achieve the Goal, it also empowers patients and providers to create personalized treatment plans and better outcomes." (*UrSure*)

* "We can all agree we want to know how we can reduce the risk of business decision-making. Despite the barriers we all know exist, the real problem is Big Data doesn't just create more knowledge, it creates more unknowns. Yet we can agree it's true that the greatest risk comes from the unknown. That's why, to achieve the goal, we need to pair Big Data with 'Thick' Data—data and insights drawn from what Big Data doesn't (and can't) track. Here's how: use people like ethnographers and researchers to collect and interpret data that can't be quantified, like stories, emotions, and interactions. Not only does that achieve the goal, it also gives companies ownable insights that could potentially improve their business and transform their industries." (*Tricia Wang*)

* "We can all agree we want to know how we can best deliver on our mission. Despite the barriers we all know exist, the real problem is the relationship between 'content output' (what and how much we produce) and 'content exposure' (who sees it, and how many). Yet we can agree it's true that the more people who see our content, the more impact it will

have. That's why, to achieve the goal, we need to adopt this project as a way to both increase who sees our content, and through the revenue it generates, increase our capacity for content output. Here's how: create a new editorial position of newsletter editor. Not only does that achieve the goal, it also creates a new potential revenue stream that would support both the editorial and financial missions of our organization." (*nonprofit media company*)

* "We can all agree we want to know how we can feel more comfortable on stage and on camera. Despite the barriers we all know exist, the real problem is seeing fear as one big thing, rather than as a collection of many things. Yet we can agree it's true that experiences leave imprints—fear leaves physical traces in our bodies. That's why, to achieve the goal, we need to address the imprints from our past experiences that are still lodged as fear in our bodies. Here's how: There are four steps: (1) Identify and deactivate past experiences. (2) Change the language we use in the stories we tell ourselves about what's happening. (3) Reconnect with the enjoyment of being the center of attention. (4) Build capacity to tolerate new, more positive feelings. Not only does that achieve the Goal, it also opens up a way for you to 'delight in the limelight' and be unapologetically *you*." (*Linda Ugelow*)

* "We can all agree we want to know what incentives will keep millennial employees from leaving.

Despite the barriers we all know exist, the real problem is focusing on positions more than the people in them. Yet we can agree it's true that people are what make positions work. That's why, to achieve the goal, we need to personalize incentives to the people in positions. Here's how: Offer options associated with different functions or job levels. For example, someone at a more junior level could choose between one day of remote work every month or one additional day of personal time off. Someone at a higher level could choose between three days of remote work or personal time off. Not only does that achieve the goal, it also drives the best and brightest performers—from any generation—to you as the new industry standard for a great place to work." (*Tracy Timm*)

* "We can all agree we want to know how to manage our fear. Despite the barriers we all know exist, the real problem is we think the answer lies in being 'fearless,' more than fearing fear itself less. Yet we can agree it's true that you're an everyday improviser—every day you have to figure out how to handle something you didn't plan for. That's why, to achieve the goal, we need to do scary stuff *on purpose*, every day. Here's how: conduct Fear Experiments, which have these components: focus, energy, action, repeat. Not only does that achieve the goal, it also means you can live a life of no regrets." (*Judi Holler*)

RED THREAD STORYLINE CRITERIA

1. The Red Thread Storyline includes your collected Red Thread statements.

2. It should make a case for your idea that your audience would understand intuitively (even if the various pieces need a bit more explanation for your audience to agree and act).

3. It should contain no unexplained jargon or "insider" language. (If you need to include a phrase or term your audience wouldn't understand intuitively, include an explanation within the storyline itself.)

* "We can all agree we want to know how to get people to perform to their potential. Despite the barriers we all know exist, the real problem is we hope for leaders while training followers, however unintentionally. Yet we can agree it's true that leadership is learned. That's why, to achieve the goal, we need to develop Multi-Level Leadership—leadership at every level. Here's how: help your team progress through each of four levels: contributor, coach, developer, pioneer. Not only does that achieve the goal, it also helps you create a culture of leadership." (*Ted Ma*)

Although I wrote a hypothetical Red Thread Storyline for De Beers in chapter 8, the company never made that full case overtly. But I love the reaction of my audiences when they hear it. They love knowing why that "diamond is forever" tagline was—and is—so powerful. In fact, they'll often begrudgingly admit that knowing the "why" doesn't reduce the power of the "case" at all, whether it applies to them directly or not. People still believe in the emotional value of their diamonds, even as they acknowledge the actual value is, well, a story they tell themselves.

"Proverb" for Power

There's one other reason De Beer's "a diamond is forever" is so powerful: *it sounds like a proverb.* We talked about proverbs in chapter 5. There, I suggested using proverbs to narrow down the concept behind your truth statement. But you can extend the power of proverbs to all your Red Thread statements by creating versions of them that sound like proverbs.

There are reasons sayings like "haste makes waste," "the second mouse gets the cheese," or even more modern mantras like "the only way out is through" stick in our collective consciousness. First, they're extremely useful shortcuts for summarizing our beliefs about ourselves or the world ("silence is golden") or for telling us what to do in it ("ask not what your country can do for you, ask what you can do for your country"). Second, they are powerfully easy to remember.

If you want your idea to also be an easy-to-remember and useful shortcut, then "proverb" it! Wherever possible, give your Red Thread statements the qualities of proverbs. What are those qualities? Here I need to give full credit to my friend and fellow storyteller Ron Ploof, whose book *The Proverb Effect* should be in every message-maker's library.[18] Ron tells us that proverbs have certain distinct qualities, namely:

* They are *short*, usually containing no more than 129 characters and a median of 7 words.

* They follow what Ron calls "the Benefit Rule," meaning the statement always benefits the receiver, your audience, and not you, the message-maker.

Mimicking the first quality is pretty straightforward: refine each Red Thread statement until it's short. Most of the time I tell my clients to make each statement fit the length of an old-school tweet: 140 characters (or less), counting spaces. That's slightly more characters than Ron's analysis shows, but hey, I'm feeling generous! If you're not sure how to achieve the Benefit Rule, there's a quick trick. It's based on a third quality of proverbs Ron discovered: they are written in the second person, present tense—they almost always include an explicit or implied "you," and are about how things are right now, not how they were.

Look at the proverbs I've shared throughout the book and see how they match up:

* Money doesn't buy happiness. (4 words, 28 characters)

* When two truths fight, only one lives. (7 words, 38 characters)

* A stitch in time saves nine. (6 words, 28 characters)

* What's good for the goose is good for the gander. (10 words, 49 characters)

* The runner and the road are one with the errand to be done. (13 words, 59 characters)

* Seeing is believing. (3 words, 20 characters)

* Haste makes waste. (3 words, 18 characters)

* The second mouse gets the cheese. (6 words, 33 characters)

* Silence is golden. (3 words, 18 characters)

* Ask not what your country can do for you, ask what you can do for your country. (17 words, 79 characters)

* The only way out is through. (6 words, 28 characters)

Notice, too, how "proverbing" is at work in several of the examples of storylines from earlier in this chapter:

* Make the invisible, visible. (4 words, 28 characters)

* Big Data doesn't just create more knowledge, it creates more unknowns. (11 words, 70 characters)

* The greatest risk comes from the unknown. (7 words, 41 characters)

* The more people who see our content, the more impact it will have. (13 words, 66 characters)

* Experiences leave imprints. (3 words, 27 characters)

* People are what make positions work. (6 words, 36 characters)

* You're an everyday improviser. (4 words, 30 characters)

* Do scary stuff on purpose, every day. (7 words, 37 characters)

* Leadership is learned. (3 words, 22 characters)

Since existing expressions often already sound like proverbs, I suggest looking at common axioms to start crafting.

→ **DO THIS**: Starting with your best versions of your Red Thread statements, edit each to give them the qualities of proverbs. (Keep your longer version, though, you may need it later!)

One final note: I find that problem, truth, and change statements benefit most from proverbing. They are, after all, the main elements of your case, so those are the points you want to be clearest and most memorable—just like proverbs.

Crafting the "Minimum Viable Case" for Your Idea

The great British statesman Winston Churchill once said that "we must learn to be equally good at what is short and sharp and what is long and tough."[19] Most of us can eventually convey the power and possibility of our ideas, given enough time. But you rarely have that kind of time. Even if you do, most people would be very happy for you to take less of it!

We've already talked about why using story and story structure is the best way to speed things up—it uploads the "code" of your idea straight into the story processors of your audience's brains. Because their brains don't have to do the work of finding the story they'd be looking for anyway, you save a ton of time.

That's one benefit of using the form of a story, but another important function of story is that it's how we humans make conclusions about cause and effect. When *x* happens and creates *y* result, story is the explanation our brains create to establish the relationship between the two. Professional storytellers know this concept well. In fact, a common refrain among novelists, playwrights, and screenwriters is that "a story is an argument." It's a case for an idea. It's the writer's explanation of why things happen the way they do.

This "story is an argument" concept is so deeply embedded that simply by finding the story of an idea (or building one from scratch), you're simultaneously building a case for it. By establishing a goal, revealing the real problem that stands in the way, highlighting a truth that forces a choice, and resolving the tension with a change and actions that lead to success, you explain not only what the idea is, but why it's important. You explain why you do what you do the way that you do it. In usually 150 words or fewer, you present your audience with the minimum possible amount of information they'd need to understand and agree with your idea.

Will your audience want more information and more detail? Usually, yes. But if they can understand and agree with your idea in principle based on the Red Thread Storyline alone? Then you know for sure that your idea is strong enough to build on.

Like a high-definition image reduced to the size of a thumbnail, in that one tiny storyline rests the full possible scale, scope, and impact of your idea.

That's why drafting and testing your Red Thread Storyline is the last "building" step of the Red Thread method. It lets you make sure that your idea works in miniature, so you can always be sure it works at scale. And if you know that, then you know your idea is strong enough to build a pitch, presentation, book, business, or even a movement on. So, let's talk about how.

How to Build Your Red Thread Storyline

In many ways, building your Red Thread Storyline is the easiest step of all. Why? Because you've already been building it up, piece by piece, as you found each of your individual Red Thread statements. All you have to do now is string those together in one big session of copy and paste (or message Mad Libs, if, as I did, you grew up with that game).

→ **DO THIS**: Gather all your other Red Thread statements from the previous chapters.

Copy and paste those statements into the storyline template (see the opening of the chapter).

Once your individual Red Thread statements are where they belong, you'll sometimes find that something doesn't quite work. Sometimes it's a "surface" issue like the language of the template or an individual statement. In that very normal situation, feel free to adjust the language of the template and/or the statement to get the fit and flow you're seeking.

TEDxCambridge speaker Dheeraj Roy, the Alzheimer's researcher I mentioned earlier, gives us a good example of this smoothing and tweaking process. You may remember in Dheeraj's case that his research provided a new truth: that it's possible to strengthen the memory retrieval system in mice with early-stage Alzheimer's. That statement doesn't work—at least not as an introduction to his idea—with a lead-in of "yet we can agree it's true that…" People can't agree that's true until he explains his research. So, Dheeraj could change the truth lead-in along the lines of, "Yet *I've discovered* that it's possible…"

→ **DO THIS**: Adjust the language of the template or your statements as needed to get a paragraph that reads smoothly and logically.

Sometimes what's "off" is something a bit deeper. When the statements are strung together, you may realize that the logic doesn't work and thus neither does

LIKE A HIGH-DEFINITION IMAGE
REDUCED TO THE SIZE OF A
THUMBNAIL, IN THAT ONE TINY
STORYLINE RESTS THE FULL
POSSIBLE SCALE, SCOPE, AND
IMPACT OF YOUR IDEA.

———————

the case for your idea. That's normal, too. When that happens, first identify which Red Thread statement isn't working (check against the criteria listed in that statement's chapter) and then rework it until you have a storyline that fits. That may mean you need to rework some of the statements that follow. That's okay, too! It's better to discover—and solve—issues with your Red Thread Storyline at this point than after you've built it into something much larger.

→ **DO THIS**: If there's an issue with one of the individual Red Thread statements, adjust it. Make sure it meets the criteria for that kind of statement and the logical flow of your Red Thread Storyline.

Adjust the statement overall as needed to fit.

Other Ways to Use the Red Thread Storyline

With practice, you might find that you can just start with the storyline to build your Red Thread. Instead of developing each piece separately, you'll just draft a storyline paragraph that articulates and argues for your idea.

Also, in my work with clients, we often "check" the strength of the Red Thread Storyline once we've defined the change. You can do this by reading your storyline out loud and asking questions like these:

- Does it make sense? Would the audience agree with each statement, as well as the overall logic?

- Does it capture the idea the way you want it to? Does it feel right to you? (This may seem like a "squishy"

THE RED THREAD STORYLINE **177**

metric, but the message has to resonate with you before it will resonate with anyone else. As a former boss used to say to me, "No one will ever be more excited about your content than you"—so make sure you're excited!)

* Do the statements allow for the longer, more nuanced, or more sophisticated explanations of the idea that longer forms of content might require? Do the Red Thread statements serve as "topic sentences" for longer explanations?

Adapting the Red Thread Storyline to Sell

You'll notice that the format of the storyline so far is one that makes the case for your *idea* more than it makes the case for *you* or your company. I always recommend to my clients that they start there, as it ensures your idea is strong enough to build on. That said, a lot of you likely have things you want to be able to do with that idea, so the idea—and thus your Red Thread and storyline—needs to sell you, too.

With some slight adaptations to the template, your storyline can work as a baseline case for you or your company—often known as an "elevator pitch" (because you can deliver it while riding on an elevator between floors).

The form of the Red Thread Storyline that you constructed at the beginning of this chapter is what I call the "explaining" version. As you'd expect, you'll use it whenever you need to explain your idea or when promoting yourself or your company wouldn't make sense. This storyline is behind most of the presentations, books, and the descriptions for each that I build with clients. If you need to use the storyline to "sell" your idea (and not just explain it), adapt the template language to feature you or your company a bit more, like this:

> We can all agree we want to know… [GOAL]. Despite the barriers we all know exist, our experience working with other people/clients like you shows the real problem is… [TWO-PART PROBLEM]. Yet we believe (or our research shows) that… [TRUTH]. That's why our answer is to… [CHANGE]. Here's how: [ACTIONS]. Not only does that achieve the goal, we find people/clients also… [GOAL REVISITED].

It's a subtle change, but an effective one for use in sales messaging, pitches, and website home or About Us pages.

Different Tenses for Different Uses

More often than not, you're drafting a Red Thread to make the case for why your idea answers your audience's question *right now*. That said, with some simple changes in tense, you can use it to describe why you did something in the past or what needs to happen in the future.

For example, with only slight adjustments, my client UrSure could adapt their Red Thread to become more of an "origin story" for their company that tells why and how they got to where they are now (I've emphasized the words with changed tense):

> When we *founded* this company, we *had* one question: "How can we keep people on critical medications longer?" Blood test results *couldn't* provide immediate answers to whether or not patients were taking their medications. As a result, we *saw* doctors *had* to rely almost exclusively on what their patients *recalled* during in-office conversations. Yet, we *believed* that "seeing is believing," so we *decided* to do something different: we *wanted* to figure out a way to make the invisible, visible, instantly—to turn the effects people can't feel into results they can see. So, we *focused* on creating simple urine tests...

Sometimes it makes sense to use the Red Thread Storyline to talk about a *future* action, usually to avoid a problem that could or will happen. Ted Ma, creator of Multi-Level Leadership, could position his Red Thread this way:

> We can all agree we want to know how to get people to perform to their potential. *But what if* we discovered we were hoping for leaders, but our actions were actually training followers, instead? *If we agree* that leadership is learned, *then we would* need to change our approach. *We'd need* to develop leadership skills in our people at every level. Here's how we *could* do that...

Positioning a Red Thread in the future like this is also a way of "defanging" bad news or framing a current problem to someone who might otherwise be unwilling to listen. (Sometimes it's easier to think through a "hypothetical" problem than an actual one!)

From Minimum Viable Case to Minimum Viable Message

With your Red Thread Storyline, you now have the minimum viable case for your message—the shortest, and strongest, articulation of your idea and why it's important. Sometimes, though, you need something that's even shorter, whether because you need something that starts a larger conversation... or because even sixty seconds is more time than you have. For that, you need a minimum viable *message*—something that allows you to finally answer the TEDx test I mentioned way back in the introduction.

For that, you'll need your Red Thread Throughline.

Steps Through the Maze (aka Action Items!)

To build the storyline of your Red Thread, have you:

☐ Strung together the Red Thread statements into the storyline template?

☐ Tweaked the language to arrive at a paragraph that reads smoothly and logically?

(10)

THE RED THREAD THROUGHLINE

GOAL: Build the story of change people will tell themselves (so you can turn your idea into action, and maybe even change the world).

PROBLEM: While your message should create questions in people's minds, those questions need to come from curiosity, not confusion.

TRUTH: What your audience learns through curiosity lasts in their worldview. It becomes part of their narrative, the story they tell themselves.

CHANGE: At every step of the way, don't just satisfy curiosity, create it.

ACTION: Draft your Red Thread Throughline.

A SMALL KEY

CAN OPEN

BIG DOORS

What Is the Red Thread Throughline?

The *Red Thread Throughline* is a one-sentence summary of your audience's question and your answer to it. Its purpose is to both satisfy your audience's curiosity and create more. Your Red Thread Throughline should comfortably answer the question, "What is your idea?"

* My idea is...
* I'm going to talk about...
* This book is about...
* Our company helps you...

Let's look at more examples of Red Thread Throughlines, all of which are under 140 characters and answer the question, "What is your idea?"

* "We keep patients on critical medications longer through simple urine tests that turn effects people can't feel into results they can see."

* "This talk is about how pairing Big Data with 'Thick' Data—human insights—can reduce the risk of business decision-making."

* "We're presenting why investing in this project helps serve both the editorial and financial missions of our organization."

- "This keynote is about how overcoming camera- and stage fright lies in addressing imprints from our past experiences that appear as fear."

- "I'm going to show you how you can keep millennial employees from leaving by personalizing incentives to the people in positions."

- "To manage your fear, do scary stuff on purpose, every day."

- "To get people to perform to their potential, develop leadership at every level."

You can, of course, apply those same criteria to our ongoing De Beers example for something like, "The best symbol of a commitment is a diamond because a diamond is forever."

Finding Your Red Thread Throughline

If there's one thing your audience *doesn't* have a lot of, it's time. That's part of the reason why, way back at the beginning of this book, I asked you to put your idea through the TEDx test. Remember that one? That's where I asked you to state your idea in a sentence of 140 characters or fewer. I gave you these guidelines:

- Use only words that someone who knows nothing about your idea would easily understand.

- Include something your audience would agree they want—out loud, in front of colleagues or friends.

* Include a new, unexpected way for the audience to achieve the goal.

With my clients, I often refer to the answer of that TEDx test as the "minimum viable message," a phrase that takes its cue from the Agile and Lean movements in start-ups and product development. Those approaches recommend what's called a "minimum viable product": "That version of a new product which allows a team to collect the maximum amount of validated learning about customers with the least effort."[20] The MVP, as it's commonly known, is never meant to be the final product. It's simply a working version of the product that allows teams and companies to figure out what's working and what isn't.

RED THREAD THROUGHLINE CRITERIA

1. The Red Thread Throughline must contain some version of your audience's goal.

2. It must also contain some aspect of the problem, truth, and/or change.

3. It can contain only words that someone who knows nothing about your idea would easily understand. If you must use proprietary terms or unusual words, you must explain them using words that someone who knows nothing about your idea already would easily understand.

4. It must be 140 characters or fewer.

When it comes to talking about your ideas, you need something that serves a similar purpose. Your Red Thread Throughline, particularly in its shortest, TEDx-test-passing form, is your minimum viable message. It allows you to put something forward about your idea to test if and how it's working to achieve your outcomes. How people respond to your Red Thread Throughline tells you a lot about the strength of your message. If someone asks you about your idea, you tell them your Red Thread Throughline, and they wander off to a different corner of the cocktail party... well, that's not good, is it?

It's also not good if someone has the courtesy to stick around and ask more questions but asks the "wrong" type of questions. All questions are not created equal. Questions that come from confusion or lack of comprehension tell you that you have more work to do on your Red Thread, and maybe even your idea itself. You don't want people to ask for more information because they don't understand what you're saying or why it's important.

Here's the source of questions that you are looking for: curiosity. You want people to ask for more information because they understand and still want to know more.

Why is curiosity so important? Because it leads to learning—and what's learned lasts. It stays in the mind of your audience and becomes part of their worldview. What your audience learns, especially when driven by their own curiosity, changes the lens through which they see the world. Sometimes those changes happen in big ways, other times in small. But each change is permanent. Just like we don't unwant or unbelieve quickly, we also don't unlearn readily... and neither does your audience. What you learn becomes part of the story you tell yourself. That's why you need to do more than simply satisfy your audience's curiosity. You need to create curiosity, too.

That's what a minimum viable message does, and now you have all you need to create it. As you've been building the minimum viable case for your idea (in the form of the Red Thread Storyline), you've been collecting ingredients that you can now combine in new, powerful ways. The most powerful form of all? The simple, short answer to the question, "What is your idea?"—your Red Thread Throughline.

It's time, finally, to find it.

How to Build Your Red Thread Throughline

To build your one-sentence Red Thread Throughline, use this formula:

> Red Thread Throughline = Goal + [Problem, Truth, and/or Change]

The Red Thread Throughline *always* includes some version of the goal. The goal makes your message relevant because it establishes what question your idea answers.

To make your message remarkable, as well, your Red Thread Throughline needs to include whatever aspect of your idea is most unexpected. That second part can be drawn from your problem, truth, or change, or even some combination.

→ **DO THIS**: Using the "formula," brainstorm each of the possible Red Thread Throughline combinations:

* Goal + Change (often the most common)
* Goal + Problem (next most common)
* Goal + Truth (least common, but still useful!)

Complete the following sentences with introductory text appropriate to your application:

* My idea is ...
* I'm going to talk about ...
* This book is about ...
* Our company helps ...

Complete your Red Thread Throughline with the best of your brainstormed combinations, making sure to meet the criteria listed above.

Sometimes the best combination of your goal with another element is obvious. Sometimes it takes a bit more brainstorming to find the one that will work best in your specific situation or application. As usual, though, keep those extra brainstorms, as those other versions of your Red Thread Throughline will likely come in handy for future applications.

HERE'S THE SOURCE OF

QUESTIONS THAT YOU ARE

LOOKING FOR: CURIOSITY. YOU

WANT PEOPLE TO ASK FOR

MORE INFORMATION BECAUSE

THEY UNDERSTAND AND STILL

WANT TO KNOW MORE.

———————

From Description, to Trailer, to Full-Length Movie

Your one-line Red Thread Throughline is like the short description of a movie you read to determine whether or not you're interested in it (often referred to as a "log-line"). If you are, you might seek out the trailer. If *that* looks interesting, then you're usually willing to watch the whole movie.

Similarly, since your Red Thread Throughline is your answer to your audience asking, "What is your idea?" (and all that question's variants), it acts like that one-line movie description. Your audience decides from there whether or not they want more. If they do, you have the "trailer": your storyline. After that comes the "movie," whatever longer form of content that makes the most sense for your application.

With your Red Thread Throughline as your minimum viable message and your storyline as your minimum viable case, you now have a powerful one-two punch for telling the story of your idea. You *also* have all the ingredients to create what your audience needs to build the story they'll tell themselves, and others, about it.

Steps Through the Maze (aka Action Items!)

To find your Red Thread Throughline, have you:

☐ Brainstormed each of the possible combinations (Goal + Change, Goal + Problem, and Goal + Truth)?

☐ Chosen and drafted your strongest option as a single sentence?

THE PAST IS
THE FUTURE OF
THE PRESENT

CONCLUSION
PUTTING YOUR RED THREAD TO WORK

AT THE beginning of this book, I told you the story of the red thread that Theseus used to defeat the Minotaur and its labyrinth. While that red thread is the origin story of the method you've just learned about, it's not the only red thread out there. In fact, there are red threads in just about every culture, religion, and philosophy. That said, knowing just a little bit more about some of the main ones can give you insight into your own Red Thread and how else you can use it.

The Red Thread of Fate

In certain Eastern philosophies, the "red thread of fate" (or sometimes, the "red thread of destiny") refers to an invisible red thread that connects you with others. Some believe it ties you to your romantic soulmate. Others apply that connection more broadly, like between a child and their adoptive parents. Either way, people believe that the thread may stretch or tangle but it never breaks.

How it applies

The red thread of fate ties to your Red Thread in how both represent a connection to other people. Remember that your Red Thread is the connection between your audience's question and the answer your idea, product, or service represents. Your aim, of course, is to keep that thread whole and untangled and your focus tied constantly to your audience.

Your idea never exists on its own. It lives in the space between you and those you want to serve. Your Red Thread is that connection, that lifeline, that makes the otherwise invisible link tangible and actionable.

The Rogue's Yarn

The "rogue's yarn" finds its roots in the golden age of sailing. Think tall ships and pirates, and you'll start to picture the kind of rogue we're talking about: those that would steal highly valuable rope for their own ships. To deter that kind of theft, or to identify the owner of the rope after it was recovered, people started to insert a colored thread to mark it as their own. Most famously, the British Royal Navy chose red for their rogue's yarns (Goethe even wrote about it in 1809)[21] and another red thread metaphor was born.

How it applies

As a career brand strategist (not to mention a fan of pirates—*aaargh*!), this particular "differentiation" red thread holds a special place in my heart. I love the idea that you can make your ideas so aligned with what or who you are that even the smallest piece of them can still be recognized as yours. The best way to do that? Root your ideas, and your case for them, in your unique combination of wants, perspectives, and beliefs, which is your Red Thread.

The Red Thread you've just built—and all the ones you will build from now on—is rooted in your worldview. By definition, your worldview is unique and different. No one else sees the world exactly as you do, because no one else has lived exactly the same life as you have. (And yes, this applies to organizations, too.)

By articulating your Red Thread, you've created something that is uniquely yours. The more you put it out in the world, the more your audience will see it and associate it with you.

Theseus's Red Thread

You should be very familiar with this last red thread by now. As I mentioned back in the introduction, this last

BY FINDING THE STORY
OF YOUR IDEA, YOU'VE
BUILT THE STORY YOUR
AUDIENCE WILL TELL
THEMSELVES, AND OTHERS,
ABOUT YOUR IDEA.

red thread is the one that inspired the name of my Red Thread system. It's the Nordic allusion to the Greek myth and refers to the core theme of something, the "logical progression of thoughts," as I once saw it defined. It is the throughline that makes it all make sense.

I don't need to tell you the story again, but I do want to point out how you've just lived it yourself: you've found your way to the center of the mental maze, to the idea that slays a monster the audience needs to fight, too. By tracing that path with your Red Thread, you've given your audience a way to take the same steps and, hopefully, reach the same conclusion. You've given them both the way and the reason to make a change and achieve their goals.

How it applies

With your Red Thread statements, the storyline that connects them, and the Red Thread Throughline that summarizes them, you now have everything you need to get your message across and your big idea out into the world.

The Power of the Red Thread

This book shows just a small sampling of the various elements and uses of a Red Thread. For many more examples, you can read my 100-plus newsletter posts, almost all of which have a very findable Red Thread running through them. (*Hint:* I often bold the Red

Thread statements.) You can also view 100-plus videos on my YouTube channel, also all containing Red Threads in various forms.

The process you've just learned and applied appears now in hundreds of messages, marketing campaigns, presentations, TED and TEDx talks, keynotes, books, and more. Those are the results of hundreds of clients, either in direct work with me or on their own, finding and building the Red Threads of their ideas. They then shaped those Red Threads to fit their applications and outcomes.

Even though the underlying structure remains the same, the variety, style, and kinds of content and conversions you can build on your Red Thread are nearly infinite. It's said, for instance, that all of storytelling has only seven basic plots. Assuming that's true, think about the huge number of and differences in all the stories in the world. It's even more amazing when you realize all those stories have the same five elements of the Red Thread: goal, problem, truth, change, action. But what ultimately fascinates me the most about finding and building Red Threads is that the more Red Threads you build, the more they connect and weave together to form the fabric of your unique worldview.

One of the most common reasons clients give for working with me is that they're trying to make sense of all the work they've done so far—for themselves and in relation to the broader market. In fact, many of them are concerned that there won't be a connection between their products, projects, initiatives, or ideas. But there *always* is. Why? Because of what the

Red Thread represents. It's how you fill in the mental "Mad Lib" of story structure. Each time you've developed an idea, created a new product or company, or even chosen a new career, your brain has been filling in the blanks.

The results may have been very different, but the one constant is ... *you*.

And that's the wild and wonderful discovery made by so many of my clients and others: by finding the Red Thread of your idea, more often than not, you end up with the Red Thread of you. You end up revealing the patterns that drive your decisions, the story that you're adding to every day, the narrative that guides your life and the work you do.

The World Needs You

You have a great idea within you. I truly believe that, and I hope you do, too. Your idea *can* change the world, because it already changed yours in some transformative way. You thought it, and then you couldn't unthink it. And now you know how to talk about your idea so that others can't unhear it. Your audience wants, and needs, an answer to their question—they want and need to achieve their goal. And now you know their brains need to follow a specific path to connect that question with the answer of your idea.

By finding the story of your idea, you've built the story your audience will tell themselves, and others, about your idea.

And while the shape of the story may be universal, how you build it, and how you tell it, is uniquely yours. Once you have it, you have a Red Thread that weaves together all three of the red threads I described above. Like Theseus, your Red Thread will help you find the shape of your story and the case for your idea. Like the Rogue's Yarn, your Red Thread reflects your distinct and differentiating point of view. And like the red thread of fate, *your* Red Thread connects you to the people you most want and need to serve.

The world needs your Red Thread. The world needs your idea. The world needs *you*.

Help us slay our monsters.

Help us save our cities.

Help us find your Red Thread, so we can weave it together with our own.

ACKNOWLEDGMENTS

ONE OF the most important rules of storytelling-as-message is to never make yourself the hero of your story. (I'm not a fan of making yourself the mentor, either, by the way!) In my experience it's far better to acknowledge that I'm only a fellow traveler. How lucky I am to have had these people with me on this road.

My sons, Thomas and Peter, have always delighted in the fact that I "make presentations to people about making presentations to people." This is what I say in those presentations, boys! And even though it will no doubt be a long time before they ever care to read this (if they ever do), the most important message I could ever deliver is that *they* are what I'm most proud of in this world. They've also helped me rethink everything I *thought* I knew about communication. Thank you, too, to their father, Patrick, the very best of co-parents and the truest of friends, even still.

Growing up, my sister and I always joked that my parents were spies, as they had jobs that needed quite a bit of explanation. The one thing that's always been crystal clear, though: their fascination with people and the world are enormous gifts and are indelibly a part of my own Red Thread. Up until this book, I was repaying that "favor" of their inscrutable careers with an equally hard-to-explain one. Now they can just say "author." Thank you for the curiosity, love, and faith that have made that evolution, and mine, possible.

Speaking of my sister, Kira's actually the true, and Emmy Award–winning, storyteller of the family. She's also saved me, both literally(!) and figuratively, and multiple times at that. This book, my business, and my life would not be possible without her and my brother-in-law, Allen. I can't ever say "thank you" enough. I will continue to try.

Melissa Case is the very best of friends, and my go-to if I ever want or need to dress up as the '80s pop group The Human League. Her Red Thread has made mine stronger in so many ways. She also makes things a heck of a lot more fun (to wit: The Human League!).

To my "person," Neen, who is truly one of the best people you could ever have in your corner. She's talked me off multiple ledges and away from multiple hippo-potamuses (long story). *Everyone* needs a Neen James. I'm so thankful I have this one. Everyone also needs a "squad" like I have in the SheNoters: Neen, Tami Evans, and Erin Gargan King. Thanks for sneaking out for snacks, ladies, and for being the source of the most supportive—and sassy—text string on the planet.

The Red Thread would not have its name were it not for a dinner that Neen and I had with two other of our brilliant friends, Joey Coleman and Clay Hebert. Thanks for helping me see the connection that was right in front of me and for their excited answer of "YES!" when I asked if the "Red Thread" was the right name for what I was working on. Seriously, when people that smart get that excited, you know you're onto something.

Ron Ploof, Laura Gassner Otting, and Diane Mulcahy were also there at, and even before, the beginning. LGO and Diane were the one-two punch that got me to start my own business. I'm grateful for that combined kick in the pants and for Laura's willingness to be one of my first official clients. She's taught me so much. My monthly conversations with Ron about our respective projects four years ago were the first and earliest tests of this idea. Ron's project, which eventually turned into his book *The Proverb Effect*, was obviously seminal in my thinking. Thank you, Ron, for teaching me how to spot, and speak, proverbs.

The Red Thread got its first tests in my work with the speakers of TEDxCambridge. I don't think Dmitri Gunn (the executive director) and I could ever have imagined what would come of the lunch we had that one day, way back when, when he suggested I might enjoy working with the speakers. Um, *yes*. In fact, that work has been, and continues to be, some of the most rewarding that I do. So, thank you, Dmitri, for being my work husband, little (and yet incredibly tall) brother, and the best riffing partner in "idea jazz."

As the very best coaches do, Michael and Amy Port helped me push through to a deeper understanding of my own idea. My own TEDx talk on the Red Thread, and even the idea itself, wouldn't be the same without them. Thank you, friends.

The brilliant and generous Mitch Joel and Jay Baer each had a critical hand in early conversations about the book and what it needed to do for you, the reader, and for me. Josh Bernoff helped me clarify what the book *wasn't* about, so thank you for that equally important contribution! The incomparable Ann Handley told me to choose a book that would be easy for me to write. While writing a book is not easy, I'm so very glad I took her advice.

When you're working on an idea and a book like this, you get a lot of feedback from people, both solicited and not. Thankfully, I have the honor of having had Majja Dennis as a boss in a former life and a friend in this current one. She taught me what is still some of the best advice I've ever gotten: "You don't get to choose how someone else interprets you. You only get to choose the experiences you offer." I think you can see how foundational that advice has been to me. Indeed, it's at the heart of the Red Thread approach this book is all about.

My soul sister and fellow tough broad Clementina Esposito helped me shape the "how" and "for whom" of the Red Thread from the beginning. I'm lucky to have such a storytelling expert, and friend, in her.

Deborah Ager was actually the very first person to officially work with me on this book. Our conversations turned into the outline of what you're reading now. Her thoughtful prodding and questioning helped make sure that subsequent editors (hopefully!) had less to do.

Kendra Ward, my editor, may take the Fifth on that (though can she? She's Canadian...). Regardless, I am honored by her ability to hold space for this idea throughout the process to create the best possible version of it.

This book is itself a testament to the faith Jesse Finkelstein and Trena White had in me. Thanks to that, their incredible team at Page Two, and their belief in what true partnerships can look like, you have this book in your hands.

Faith is nothing without a good plan, and good friends, to back it up. For that I'm blessed to have two such friends and advisers. Pamela Slim truly is friend first and business coach second. Thanks for wiping all the virtual tears (and actual tears, virtually). In that role she is joined by Wendi Hall, who at this point is second only to my sister in the decidedly unglamorous role of helping me work my way out of trouble. She once sent me a mug that said, "Sometimes you forget you're awesome, so this is your reminder." *You're* awesome, Wendi. This is a reminder.

My friend and client Jennifer Iannolo once called me "the Idea Whisperer," a moniker that has, to my eternal delight, stuck. But there's one other person without whom none of that, or this—in the form of this book or my business—would exist: Jennifer Montfort. She calls herself "the Tamsen Whisperer," and truer words were never spoken. She first worked with me over a decade ago, and even when our professional lives led us in different directions, she was always at the top of my list for when I wanted to build a team of my own. And now, she *is* my team. She, truly, is the one that runs everything, makes sure our clients get what they need, and helps me keep my head on straight. And she does all of this with the most beautiful, genuine soul you could ever hope to meet. I quite literally could not do any of what I do without her.

And finally, Tom, my husband, other half, and constant beam. He has believed in me, and this idea, from the beginning, *especially* when I didn't. No doubt I could have done all this alone, but I'm sure glad I didn't have to. Here's to forty good years, and to partners. Thank you for being mine.

NOTES

1. Tricia Wang, "The Human Insights Missing from Big Data," filmed September 2016 at TEDxCambridge, Boston, MA, video, ted.com/talks/tricia_wang_the_human_insights_missing_from_big_data.
2. Simon Sinek, "How Great Leaders Inspire Action," filmed September 2009 at TEDxPugetSound, Newcastle, WA, video, ted.com/talks/simon_sinek_how_great_leaders_inspire_action.
3. Manda Mahoney, "How Customers Think: The Subconscious Mind of the Consumer (and How to Reach It)," *Working Knowledge* (Harvard Business School), January 13, 2003, hbswk.hbs.edu.
4. Chip Heath and Dan Heath, *Made to Stick: Why Some Ideas Survive and Others Die* (New York: Random House Publishing Group, 2007), Introduction, Kindle.
5. Blaise Pascal, *Pascal's Pensées* (New York: E.P. Dutton & Co., 1958), section I, released April 27, 2006, Project Gutenberg eBook, gutenberg.org/files/18269/18269-h/18269-h.htm.
6. A. Gopnik et al., *The Scientist in the Crib* (New York: Harper Perennial, 1999), quoted in Kendall Haven, *Story Proof: The Science behind the Startling Power of Story* (Westport, CT: Libraries Unlimited, 2007), chap. 4, Kindle.
7. Janice Chen et al., "Shared Memories Reveal Shared Structure in Neural Activity across Individuals," *Nature Neuroscience* 20 (2017): 115-25, doi.org/10.1038/nn.4450.

8. Nick Morgan, *Power Cues: The Subtle Science of Leading Groups, Persuading Others, and Maximizing Your Personal Impact* (Boston: Harvard Business Review Press, 2014), chap. 7, Kindle.

9. Bill Schley, *The Micro-Script Rules: It's Not What People Hear. It's What They Repeat...* (New York: WidenerBooks, 2010), chap. 5, Kindle.

10. Susan Weinschenk, *100 Things Every Presenter Needs to Know about People* (Berkeley, CA: New Riders, 2012), chap. 15, Kindle.

11. Taiichi Ohno, *Toyota Production System: Beyond Large-Scale Production* (Boca Raton, FL: CRC Press, 1988), Glossary, Kindle.

12. Barry Schwartz, *The Paradox of Choice: Why More Is Less*, works.swarthmore.edu/fac-psychology/198.

13. "The 4 Cs," De Beers, debeers.com.

14. Maggie Seaver, "Do People Still Follow the 3 Months' Salary Rule for Engagement Rings?," The Knot, theknot.com.

15. Neen James, *Attention Pays: How to Drive Profitability, Productivity, and Accountability* (Hoboken, NJ: John Wiley & Sons, 2018), Kindle.

16. Shawn Coyne, *The Story Grid: What Good Editors Know* (New York: Black Irish Entertainment, 2015), chap. 25, Kindle.

17. Seth Godin, *Free Prize Inside: The Next Big Marketing Idea* (New York: Portfolio, 2004).

18. Ron Ploof, *The Proverb Effect: Secrets to Creating Tiny Phrases That Change the World* (self-pub., 2008).

19. Sir Winston Churchill, under "Perseverance" in *Churchill by Himself: In His Own Words,* ed. Richard M. Langworth (Rosetta Books, 2013), chap. 1, Kindle.

20. "Minimum Viable Product (MVP)," Glossary, Agile Alliance, agilealliance.org.

21. Johann Wolfgang von Goethe, *Die Wahlverwandtschaften* [*The Elective Affinities*] (1809, in German), chap. 2, updated April 17, 2020, Project Gutenberg eBook, gutenberg.org/files/2403/2403-h/2403-h.htm.

ABOUT THE AUTHOR

TAMSEN WEBSTER has spent the last twenty years helping experts drive action from their ideas. Part message strategist, part storyteller, part English-to-English translator, her work focuses on how to find and build the stories partners, investors, clients, and customers will tell themselves—and others.

Tamsen honed her expertise through work in and for major companies and organizations such as Johnson & Johnson, Harvard Medical School, and Intel, as well as with start-ups that represent the next wave of innovation in life science, biotech, climate tech, fintech, and pharma. For over seven years, she's served as executive producer and idea strategist for one of the oldest locally organized TED talk events in the world (TEDxCambridge).

Tamsen was a reluctant marathoner... twice; is a champion ballroom dancer (in her mind); and learned everything she knows about messages, people, and change as a Weight Watchers leader. True story.

FIND YOUR RED THREAD

By now, I hope you're well on your way to finding and telling the story that is your Red Thread (not to mention changing the world). That said, if you're looking for what to do next, I'm happy to say there's nothing I like more than helping people just like you uncover all the best parts of your big ideas and helping you get them out into the world.

Here are a few ways to get started.

Copies for Your Team or Organization

Want to buy multiple copies of the book to share with your team, agency, or organization? Contact me about bulk discounts and special offers—direct to you from me—tailored to your numbers and needs.

Consulting and Team Training Sessions

If you'd like direct one-on-one help developing your or your organization's Red Thread, I have several packages and training options available. We typically start with a Red Thread Session, a series of one-on-one virtual calls where we walk through the entire Red Thread process together, including turning your Red Thread into a short-from piece of content (think: sales or pitch discussion document, website home page, book back cover copy, etc.). From there, follow-on work can include adapting your Red Thread for different audiences and use cases and training your team to incorporate your personalized Red Thread in their work.

Speaking Bundles

If you liked the concepts in this book, why not share them more broadly with your event, audience, or team? I am available to speak on any of the concepts in the book from many different perspectives, tailored—in the spirit of the Red Thread—to your audience, needs, and goals. Speaking packages span everything from a straightforward keynote with book bundle incentives to completely individualized engagements that include helping you find your Red Thread, incorporating that Red Thread into a fully customized keynote, and then training your team on how to apply your Red Thread in their work.

Red Thread Mastermind and Accreditation

Twice a year, I offer a Red Thread Mastermind program, a three-month group coaching program designed to teach you the basics of finding and building your own

Red Thread. If you want to go even deeper with the Red Thread, the Red Thread Accreditation program is for those who need to regularly find and build multiple Red Threads either for your clients or for your own organization. Typically that includes people in creative agencies, fundraising and development offices, marketing and communication teams, and even coaches and consultants. The program is open to anyone who has already worked with me to find their or their organization's Red Thread and is designed to teach you how to work with others to do the same. I offer Red Thread Accreditation to previous Mastermind or private clients once a year and as a private, customized program within your agency or organization.

Start the Conversation

I can't wait to hear about your Red Thread and to work with you toward your and your organization's success. Please reach out and we'll get started!

tamsenwebster.com/contact
hello@tamsenwebster.com
Twitter: @tamadear
FB: facebook.com/TamsenWebster
LI: linkedin.com/in/TamsenWebster
Insta: @tamsenwebster
Medium: @TamsenWebster
YouTube: youtube.com/tamsenwebster